W9-BLW-951

THE BLACK BOX

THE BLACK BOX

Cockpit Voice Recorder
Accounts of Nineteen
In-Flight Accidents

EDITED BY MALCOLM MacPHERSON

QUILL
New York   1984

Copyright © 1984 by Malcolm MacPherson

All rights reserved. No part of this book may be reproduced
or utilized in any form or by any means, electronic or mechanical,
including photocopying, recording or by any information storage
and retrieval system, without permission in writing from the
Publisher. Inquiries should be addressed to Quill, an imprint of
William Morrow and Company, Inc., 105 Madison Avenue, New York, N.Y. 10016.

Library of Congress Catalog Card Number: 84-60450

ISBN: 0-688-03294-X

Printed in the United States of America

First Quill Edition

1 2 3 4 5 6 7 8 9 10

BOOK DESIGN BY BERNARD SCHLEIFER

Acknowledgments

I AM GRATEFUL TO G. Gardner Brown in London and Brad Dunbar at the National Transportation Safety Board in Washington, D.C.

Contents

Introduction

NEARLY EVERYONE WHO has flown has experienced the fear of flying. Whether in clear skies or turbulent, during a routine flight or in an emergency, we have shared a common experience of moistened palms, white knuckles, and a wildly racing heart. What lies behind our fear is the essential loss of control, the utter blind faith with which we entrust our lives to two or three complete strangers who sit behind a closed door in the airplane's cockpit. Against those faceless men are arrayed the mysterious, violent, unpredictable forces of nature, the millions of components in the aircraft (without the proper manufacture or repair of which and we fall out of the sky) and, of course, the scores of electronic and human eyes on the ground that should be watching our progress.

No evidence can seem to dispel this fear. When a storm violently buffets the airframe in which we are riding, no recitation of safety statistics will quiet the heart. Still, besides walking, the safest way to travel anywhere is aboard a commercial airliner. Thanks largely to the high level of professionalism among the airlines' personnel, the Federal Aviation Administration, and the National Transportation Safety Board, aviation accident statistics continue on a steady downward trend: There were no fatal accidents in 1980, a mere four single-fatality accidents in 1981, in 1982 there were five fatal accidents, and in 1983 there were three. Looked at from a different perspective, there were 6.1 fatal accidents for every 10 *million* hours flown in 1981, 6.2 in the same 10 million hours in 1982, and in 1983 that figure decreased to 4.6 fatal accidents per 10 million hours. By way of contrast, 44,000 Americans died on the nation's highways last year in so many accidents that nobody bothered to count.

The industry spends an extraordinary amount of time and energy to reassure passengers with more tangible means than facts and figures. There are obvious practical reasons behind seat belts, no smoking, and straight seat backs during the critical flight periods of takeoff and landing, and the cabin crews do not repeat procedures with oxygen masks, flotation devices, and emergency exits without the certain awareness that these measures can prevent accidents and save lives, but these measures also serve to make us feel as if we hold in our hands a modicum of control over our fate. So it is also with the pilot, who reassures us often in soothing, authoritative tones, even when—especially when—he is frenzied with an emergency.

At such times as these we may feel serene, while behind the forward-bulkhead door there is another reality we do not ever see. Usually when things go wrong in the air, they go wrong all at once, as one crippled and failed system collapses on another. Suddenly, horns sound in the cockpit to warn of an equipment failure, while recorded voices shout ("Pull up! Pull up!" is repeated when the altitude minimums are violated) in the pilot's ear and lights flash in front of his eyes. Often, confusion results; automatic responses are triggered. And in a truly amazing number of incidents, the crews bring their aircraft safely home, without the passengers knowing that their lives had been in such jeopardy.

Sometimes—in a tiny percentage of flights—events do not conclude so well, and the only record we have of what has happened is contained in the shatter-proof "black box," which federal authorities have required since 1957 as standard equipment aboard all commercial aircraft over a certain weight. Actually, the box is a bright Day-Glo orange and has two components: One, the Flight Data Recorder (FDR), keeps constant track of the airplane's heading, airspeed, altitude, vertical acceleration, and microphone keying, among other things. The second component, required by law in commercial aircraft since 1966, is the Cockpit Voice Recorder (CVR), which tapes all conversations within the cockpit and between the cockpit and the ground. The CVR is a self-erasing, thirty-minute loop: Most accidents in the air occur from start to finish in less than a half hour.

I first started reading CVR transcriptions in the belief that the more I knew the less I might fear flying. Now, I try to read the complete findings of the National Transportation Safety Board for every commercial airplane accident, and nothing has given me a better feel for what things are like when things go wrong. Unfortunately, reading the CVR transcripts has done nothing to allay my basic and persistent fears of flying, although they do go a long way to explain in the most graphic manner the professionalism—if not the downright heroism—of many commercial pilots and crews and the extraordinary measures they take to ensure our—the passengers'—safety.

I have made no effort to "characterize" the crew members whose voices are taken directly from these CVR tapes. Whether the captain is kind to animals, is married with children, et cetera, does not seem relevant in an accident environment. While I edited some dialogue for easier understanding, the reader should feel that he has tuned his radio at home into an emergency channel and is overhearing the conversations between the crew members in the airplane cockpit and the ground controllers during an emergency. Even though you may not be able to visualize everything that is happening, I think you will agree that the transcripts are as dramatic reading as you are likely to find, because they are the minute-by-minute unvarnished accounts of what actually happened.

—M. MacPherson

New York, 1984

1. Southern Airways Flight 242 (SOU 242)

On 4 April 1977, Southern Airways Flight 242, a DC-9-31, was operating as a scheduled passenger flight from Muscle Shoals, Alabama, to Atlanta, Georgia, with a stop at Huntsville, Alabama. About 1554 Eastern Standard Time, Flight 242 departed Huntsville on an Instrument Flight Rules (IFR) flight plan for the Hartsfield–Atlanta International Airport. There were eighty-one passengers and four crew members aboard. The flight's route was direct to the Rome VOR (a very high frequency omnidirectional range navigational aid located about forty-six miles northwest of the Atlanta airport, near the town of Rome, Georgia) and then a Rome-to-Runway 26 descent to Atlanta International. Its estimated time en route was twenty-five minutes and its requested altitude was 17,000 feet.

1541:45

STEWARDESS 1:	Is it going to be bad again from here to Atlanta?
CAPTAIN:	Ma'am?
STEWARDESS 1:	What is it going to be like from here to Atlanta?
CAPTAIN:	Just like it was coming up here. . . .
STEWARDESS 1:	Going to have to keep ourselves in our chairs, huh?
CAPTAIN:	Depends on how many people you got. We only have about . . . ten minutes level.
STEWARDESS 2:	(GREETING PASSENGERS IN CABIN.)
STEWARDESS 1:	Do you need anything [to the crew in cockpit]?
FIRST OFFICER:	Yeah, I want a good . . . ah . . . well done.
STEWARDESS 1:	Tell you later, really [if she had the meal requested].

FIRST OFFICER:	Well done [on the food].
STEWARDESS 1:	Where do you live at?
FIRST OFFICER:	La Place.
STEWARDESS 1:	Where is that? Oh, you go to the right?
FIRST OFFICER:	Yeah, I go to the right.
STEWARDESS 1:	I think Cathy will give me a ride. I didn't realize I was late for a minute. I was so lucky to even be here . . . just spent eighteen dollars to get my hair done. . . .
CAPTAIN:	You ought to be proud you got some hair. I don't have any hair. I don't care what color it is, just so I get some hair.
STEWARDESS 1:	Really?
CAPTAIN:	Do we change airplanes going . . . ?
STEWARDESS 1:	Sure, you don't think . . . we're going to make this trip as difficult as possible?
FIRST OFFICER:	God, we're in and out of Atlanta three times in one day and we change airplanes three times in one day. . . .
CAPTAIN:	Yep. (PRETAXI SAFETY INSTRUCTIONS TO PASSENGERS ON PA [PUBLIC ADDRESS] INTERCOM.)
FIRST OFFICER:	Thank you, sir. See you later. (AGENT ON THE GROUND, "SEE YOU.") Here, Bill, Atlanta is twenty-seven hundred broken, five thousand broken, twenty-five overcast and fifteen, and gusts, and the winds are thirty-one miles an hour. Peaks are forty-seven. Who's got the landing?
CAPTAIN:	Not me.
FIRST OFFICER:	Ignition, sir.
CAPTAIN:	It's starting to rain here now.
FIRST OFFICER:	Quit raining.
CAPTAIN:	Eighty-one folk [on board] . . . four minutes late . . .
GROUND CREW:	Cockpit, Ground.
CAPTAIN:	Yes?
FIRST OFFICER:	Ignition set.
GROUND CREW:	Prepare to start Number Two. I'm going to be off the headset here a minute. I'm going to shut that [cabin] door. (STEWARDESS ANNOUNCES TWENTY-EIGHT MINUTES EN ROUTE TO ATLANTA AND FEDERAL REGULATIONS.)
GROUND CREW:	Okay, clear on one.

FIRST OFFICER: Looks like you guys got a good one [storm] coming.

GROUND CREW: Have a good one.

CAPTAIN: Two good ones.

FIRST OFFICER: Two good starts

GROUND CREW: Roger, I hold your hand signal.

FIRST OFFICER: Okay.

1550:25

FIRST OFFICER: (SOUND OF WINDSHIELD WIPERS.) Set your horizon.

CAPTAIN: [Set] your horizon when we're through the weather.

FIRST OFFICER: Flaps, Bill. Flight controls, circuit breaker, flaps thirty degrees one ninety-five, a hundred radar, you got that? Radios are on.

CAPTAIN: There's thirty, sir. I got to call ol' Steve Banks and tell him I want to give up my early morning trip Wednesday.

1552:11

FIRST OFFICER: Huntsville, 242, times are forty, forty-two, fifty-one, and fifty-four.

1552:23

COMPANY RADIO [THE AIRLINE'S LOCAL OFFICE]: Understand forty, forty-two, fifty-one, fifty-three.

1552:27

FIRST OFFICER: No, fifty-four was that very last one.

1552:31

COMPANY RADIO: Fifty-four, roger.

1552:42

HUNTSVILLE TOWER: 242, Huntsville Tower, cleared for takeoff.

1552:45

FIRST OFFICER: 242, cleared for takeoff. (SOUND OF WINDSHIELD WIPERS DURING THE FOLLOWING PERIOD.)

1553:37

CAPTAIN: Spooled and stable.

1553:38
FIRST OFFICER: Rog.

1553:45
CAPTAIN: Takeoff power is set.

1553:54
CAPTAIN: Got eighty, looking for twenty, one twenty-seven.
FIRST OFFICER: . . . Twenty-seven.

1554:04
CAPTAIN: One rotate. (SOUND OF VIBRATION.) Positive rate.
FIRST OFFICER: Gear up. (SOUND OF TRIM; SOUND OF WINDSHIELD WIPER STOPPING; SOUND OF TRIM.)

1554:22
HUNTSVILLE TOWER: 242 contact Departure, good day.

1554:25
CAPTAIN: Good day, now. Departure, Southern 242, runway heading.

1554:39
HUNTSVILLE DEPARTURE: Southern 242, Huntsville radar contact, ah, turn left heading one two zero, vector around restricted area, climb and maintain one seven thousand.

1554:38
CAPTAIN: Okay, one seven thousand heading turn left to one two zero. (CLICK OF MIKE.)
FIRST OFFICER: Flaps up, Bill.

1555:05
FIRST OFFICER: Slats up, climb check.

1555:14
HUNTSVILLE DEPARTURE: Southern 242 is clear restricted area, continue left turn, resume own navigation direct to Rome.

1555:21
CAPTAIN: Okay, direct Rome, 242.

1555:31
CAPTAIN (TO FIRST OFFICER):   I don't know what direction Rome is.

1555:34

FIRST OFFICER: About one hundred and ten [degrees].

CAPTAIN: (SOUND OF SNEEZE.) Excuse me.

FIRST OFFICER: Bless you.

1555:58

CAPTAIN: Well, the radar is full of it [foul weather], take your pick.

1556:00

HUNTSVILLE DEPARTURE: Southern 242, I'm painting a line of weather which appears to be moderate to, ah, possibly heavy precipitation starting about, ah, five miles ahead and it's . . .

1556:14

CAPTAIN: Okay, ah, we're in the rain right now, ah—it doesn't look much heavier than what we're in, does it?

1556:22

HUNTSVILLE DEPARTURE: Ah, it's painting—I got weather cutting devices on, which is cutting out the, ah, precip that you're in now. This, ah, showing up on radar, however, it doesn't. . . . It's not a solid mass, it, ah, appears to be a little bit heavier than what you're in right now.

1556:34

CAPTAIN: Okay, thank you.

1556:37

FIRST OFFICER: I can't read that. It just looks like rain, Bill. What do you think? There's a hole [in the weather].

1556:40

CAPTAIN: There's a hole right here. That's all I see. Then coming over we had pretty good radar. I believe right straight ahead, ah, there the next few miles is about the best way we can go. Rome's fifteen twenty.

FIRST OFFICER: Yeah.

1557:06

HUNTSVILLE DEPARTURE: Southern 242, squawk five six two three.

1557:15

CAPTAIN: 242, roger. [To First Officer]: If it gets rough, how about hand flying?

1557:36

HUNTSVILLE
DEPARTURE:

Southern 242, you're in what appears to be about the heaviest part of it now. What are your flight conditions?

1557:42

CAPTAIN:

Ah, we're getting a little light turbulence now and, ah, I'd say moderate rain.

1557:47

HUNTSVILLE
DEPARTURE:

Okay, and, ah, what I'm painting, it won't get any worse than that and, ah, contact Memphis Center on one two zero point eight.

1557:55

CAPTAIN:

Twenty point eight, good day now and thank you much.

1558:10

CAPTAIN:

Memphis Center, Southern, ah, 242 is with you climbing to one seven thousand.

1558:16

MEMPHIS:

Southern 242, Memphis Center, roger.

1558:22

CAPTAIN (TO FIRST
OFFICER):

As long as it doesn't get any heavier, we'll be all right.

FIRST OFFICER:

Yeah, this is good.

1558:26

MEMPHIS:

Attention all aircraft, SIGMET, hazardous weather vicinity Tennessee, southeastern Louisiana, Mississippi, northern and western Alabama and adjacent coastal waters, monitor VOR broadcast within a hundred-fifty-mile radius of the SIGMET area.

1558:41

CAPTAIN:

Southeast Louisiana . . .

1558:45

MEMPHIS:

Southern 242, contact Atlanta Center, one three four point zero five.

1558:50

CAPTAIN:

Thirty-four zero five, 242, good day.

1558:54

MEMPHIS:

Good day.

1559:00
CAPTAIN (TO FIRST OFFICER): Here we go [into turbulence]. . . . Hold 'em cowboy. [To Atlanta]: Atlanta Center, Southern 242, we're out of eleven for seventeen.

1559:11
ATLANTA: Southern 242, Atlanta Center roger, expect Rome Runway 26 profile descent.

1559:16
CAPTAIN: Expect Rome 26.

1603:20
CAPTAIN: Atlanta, Southern 242, with you level seventeen.

1603:34
ATLANTA: Southern 242, Atlanta, roger altimeter two niner five six.

1603:29
CAPTAIN: Roger, two nine five six.

1603:48
CAPTAIN (TO FIRST OFFICER): Looks heavy. Nothing's going through that [weather]. See that?

1603:56
FIRST OFFICER: That's a hole, isn't it?

1603:57
CAPTAIN: It's not showing a hole, see it?

1604:08
FIRST OFFICER: Do you want to go around that right now?

1604:19
CAPTAIN: Hand fly at about two eighty-five knots

FIRST OFFICER: Two eight five. (SOUND OF HAIL AND RAIN.)

1604:50
CAPTAIN: Southern 242, we're slowing it up here a little bit.

ATLANTA: 242, roger.

1605:53
FIRST OFFICER (TO CAPTAIN): Which way do we go, 'cross here or go out . . . ? I don't know how we get through there, Bill.

CAPTAIN: I know. You're just gonna have to go out. . . .

FIRST OFFICER: Yeah, right across that band.

1606:01

CAPTAIN: All clear left, approximately, right now. I think we can cut across there now.

1606:12

FIRST OFFICER: All right, here we go. We're picking up some ice, Bill.

CAPTAIN: We are above ten degrees.

FIRST OFFICER: Right at ten.

1606:42

ATLANTA: Southern 242, descend and maintain one four thousand at this time. Southern 242, descend and maintain one four thousand.

1606:53

CAPTAIN: 242, down to fourteen.

ATLANTA: Affirmative. Southern 242, Atlanta altimeter two niner five six and cross forty miles northwest of Atlanta two five zero knots. (HEAVY HAIL OR RAIN SOUND STARTS AND CONTINUES UNTIL POWER INTERRUPTION.)

1607:22

STEWARDESS ON PA: Keep your seat belts on and securely fastened. There's nothing to be alarmed about. Relax. We should be out of it shortly.

1607:31

ATLANTA: Southern 242, what's your speed now? Southern 242, Atlanta, what's your speed?

1607:57

[Power interruption for thirty-six seconds.]

1608:33

[Power restored.] (SOUND OF RAIN CONTINUES FOR FORTY SECONDS.)

1608:34

ATLANTA: Southern 242, Atlanta.

1608:37

FIRST OFFICER: Got it [power], got it back, Bill, got it back, got it back.

1608:38
STEWARDESS
ON PA:

. . . Check to see that all carry-on baggage is stowed completely underneath the seat in front of you, all carry-on baggage . . . put all carry-on baggage underneath the seat in front of you; in the unlikely event that there is need for an emergency landing, we do ask that you please grab your ankles. I will scream from the rear of the aircraft. There is nothing to be alarmed about but we have lost temporary APU [Auxiliary Power Unit] power at times, so in the event there is any unlikely need for an emergency, you do hear us holler, please grab your ankles. Thank you for your cooperation and just relax. These are precautionary measures only.

1608:42
CAPTAIN:

Ah, 242, stand by.

1608:46
ATLANTA:

Say again.

1608:48
CAPTAIN:

Stand by.

1608:49
ATLANTA:

Roger, maintain one five thousand, if you understand me, maintain one five thousand, Southern 242.

1608:55
CAPTAIN:

We're trying to get it up there.

1608:57
ATLANTA:

Roger.

1609:15
CAPTAIN:

Okay, ah, 242, ah, we just got our windshield busted and, ah, we'll try to get it back up to fifteen. We're fourteen.

1609:25
ATLANTA:

Southern 242, you say you're at fourteen now?

1609:27
CAPTAIN:

Yeah, ah, couldn't help it.

1609:30
ATLANTA:

That's okay, ah, are you squawking five six two three?

1609:36

FIRST OFFICER (TO CAPTAIN): Left engine won't spool.

1609:37

CAPTAIN (TO ATLANTA): Our left engine just cut out.

1609:42

ATLANTA: Southern 242, roger, and, ah, lost your transponder. Squawk five six two three.

1609:43

FIRST OFFICER: I am squawking five six two three. Tell him I'm level fourteen.

1609:49

CAPTAIN: Five six two three, we're squawking.

1609:53

ATLANTA: Say you lost an engine and, ah, busted a windshield?

1609:56

CAPTAIN: Yes, sir.

1609:59

CAPTAIN: Autopilot's off. . . .

FIRST OFFICER: I've got it. I'll hand fly it.

1610:00

ATLANTA: Southern 242, you can descend and maintain one three thousand now. That'll get you down a little lower.

1610:04

FIRST OFFICER: The other engine's going [out] too!

1610:05

CAPTAIN (TO ATLANTA): Got the other engine going too.

1610:08

ATLANTA: Southern 242, say again.

1610:10

CAPTAIN: Stand by. . . . We lost both engines.

1610:14

FIRST OFFICER: All right, Bill, get us a vector to a clear area.

1610:16
CAPTAIN: Get us a vector to a clear area, Atlanta.

1610:20
ATLANTA: Ah, continue present southeasternbound heading. TWA's off to your left about fourteen miles at fourteen thousand and says he's in the clear.

1610:25
CAPTAIN: Okay. Want us to turn left?

1610:30
ATLANTA: Southern 242, contact Approach Control one two six point nine and they'll try to get you straight into Dobbins.

1610:36
FIRST OFFICER: Give me . . . I'm familiar with Dobbins. Tell them to give me a vector to Dobbins, if they're clear.

1610:38
CAPTAIN: Give me, ah, vector to Dobbins if they're clear.

1610:41
ATLANTA: Southern 242, one twenty-six point nine. They'll give you a vector to Dobbins.

1610:45
CAPTAIN: Twenty-six nine, okay.

1610:50
FIRST OFFICER: Ignition override, it's gotta work, by God. . . .

1610:56
                                [Power interruption for two minutes and four seconds.]

1613:00
                                [Power restored.]

1613:03
CAPTAIN: There we go.

1613:03.5
FIRST OFFICER: Get us a vector to Dobbins.

1613:04
CAPTAIN: Ah, Atlanta, you read Southern 242?

1613:08

ATLANTA
  APPROACH:

Southern 242, Atlanta Approach Control, ah, go ahead.

1613:11

CAPTAIN:

Ah, we've lost both engines. How about giving us a vector to the nearest place. We're at seven thousand feet.

1613:17

ATLANTA:

Southern 242, roger, turn right heading one zero zero, will be vectors to Dobbins for a straight-in approach runway, altimeter two niner five two. Your position is fifteen, correction, twenty miles west of Dobbins at this time.

1613:17

STEWARDESS ON
  PA:

Ladies and gentlemen, please check that your seat belts are securely again across your pelvis area on your hips.

FIRST OFFICER:

What's Dobbins weather, Bill? How far is it? How far is it?

1613:35

ATLANTA:

Ah, make a heading of one two zero, Southern 242, right turn to one two zero.

FIRST OFFICER:

Declare an emergency, Bill.

1613:40

CAPTAIN:

Okay, right turn to one two zero and, ah, you got us our squawk, haven't you, on emergency?

1613:45

ATLANTA:

Ah, I'm not receiving it but radar contact your position is twenty miles west of Dobbins.

1613:50

CAPTAIN:

Okay.

1614:03

FIRST OFFICER:

Get those engines . . .

1614:24

FIRST OFFICER:

All right, listen, we've lost both engines, and, ah, I can't, ah, tell you the implications of this, ah, we, ah, only got two engines and how far is Dobbins now?

1614:34
ATLANTA: Southern, ah, 242, ah, nineteen miles.

1614:40
CAPTAIN: Okay, we're out of, ah, fifty-eight hundred, two hundred knots.

1614:44
FIRST OFFICER: What's our speed, let's see, what's our weight, Bill. Get me a bug speed.

1614:45
ATLANTA: Southern 242, do you have one engine running now?

1614:48
CAPTAIN: Negative, no engines.

1614:50
ATLANTA: Roger.

1614:59
CAPTAIN: One twenty-six.

FIRST OFFICER: One twenty-six. (SOUND OF TRIM NOISE.)

1615:04
CAPTAIN: Just don't stall this thing out.

FIRST OFFICER: No, I won't.

CAPTAIN: Get your wing flaps. (SOUND OF LEVER MOVEMENT.)

1615:11
FIRST OFFICER: Got it, got hydraulics.

CAPTAIN: We got hydraulics.

1615:18
CAPTAIN (TO ATLANTA): What's your Dobbins weather?

1615:22
ATLANTA: Stand by. Southern 242, Dobbins weather is two thousand scattered, estimated ceiling three thousand broken, seven thousand overcast, visibility seven miles.

1615:57
CAPTAIN: Okay, we're down to forty-six hundred now.

1615:59
FIRST OFFICER: How far is it? How far is it?

1616:00
ATLANTA: Roger, and you're approximately, ah, seventeen miles west of Dobbins at this time.

1616:05
CAPTAIN: I don't know whether we can make that or not.

1616:07
ATLANTA: Roger.

1616:11
FIRST OFFICER: Ah, ask him if there's anything between here and Dobbins.

CAPTAIN: What?

FIRST OFFICER: Ask him if there is anything between here and Dobbins.

1616:25
CAPTAIN: Ah, is there any airport between our position and Dobbins, ah . . . ?

1616:28
STEWARDESS 1:   Sandy?

STEWARDESS 2:   Yeah?

STEWARDESS 1:   They would not talk to me. When I looked in, the whole front windshield is cracked. Okay? So what do we do?

STEWARDESS 2:   Ah, have they said anything?

STEWARDESS 1:   Ah, he screamed at me when I opened the door, ''Just sit down,'' so I didn't ask him a thing. I don't know the results or anything. I'm sure we decompressed.

STEWARDESS 2:   Ah, yes, we've lost an engine. . . .

STEWARDESS 1:   I thought so.

STEWARDESS 2:   Okay, Kathy, have you briefed all your passengers in the front?

STEWARDESS 1:   Yes, I told them I checked the cockpit and help me take the door down.

STEWARDESS 2:   Have you removed your shoes?

STEWARDESS 1:   No, I haven't.

STEWARDESS 2:	Take off your shoes. Be sure to stow them somewhere right down in the galley, in a compartment in there with the napkins or something.
STEWARDESS 1:	I got them behind the seat, so that's no good.
STEWARDESS 2:	It might keep the seat down now.
STEWARDESS 1:	Okay.
STEWARDESS 2:	Right down in one of those closets. I took off my socks so I'd have more ground pull with my toes, okay?
STEWARDESS 1:	You'd have what?
STEWARDESS 2:	So I took off my socks, so I wouldn't be sliding.
STEWARDESS 1:	Yeah.
STEWARDESS 2:	Okay?
STEWARDESS 1:	That's a good idea too.
STEWARDESS 2:	Okay.
STEWARDESS 1:	Thank you, bye-bye.

1616:29
ATLANTA: Southern 242, ah, no sir, ah, closest airport is Dobbins.

1616:34
CAPTAIN: I doubt we're going to make it, but we're trying everything to get something started.

1616:38
ATLANTA: Roger. Well, there is Cartersville. You're approximately ten miles south of Cartersville, fifteen miles west of Dobbins.

1616:44
FIRST OFFICER: We'll take a vector to that, yes, we'll have to go there.

1616:45
CAPTAIN: Can you give us a vector to Cartersville?

1616:47
ATLANTA: All right, turn left, heading of three six zero be directly, ah, direct vector to Cartersville.

1616:52
CAPTAIN: Three six zero, roger.

FIRST OFFICER: What runway? What's the heading on the runway?

1616:53
CAPTAIN: What's the runway heading?

1616:58
ATLANTA: Stand by.

1616:59
CAPTAIN: And how long is it?

1617:00
ATLANTA: Stand by.

1617:08
CAPTAIN: Like we are, I'm picking out a clear field.

1617:12
FIRST OFFICER: Bill, you've got to find me a highway [to land on].
CAPTAIN: Let's get the next clear open field.

1617:35
CAPTAIN: See a highway over . . . no cars.
FIRST OFFICER: Right there, is that straight?

1617:39
CAPTAIN: No.
FIRST OFFICER: We'll have to take it.

1617:44
ATLANTA: Southern 242, the runway configuration . . . at Cartersville is, ah, three six zero and running north and south and the elevation is seven-hundred-fifty-six feet and, ah, trying to get the length of now——it's three-thousand-two-hundred feet long.

1618:02
CAPTAIN: Ah, we're putting it on the highway . . . we're down to nothing.

1618:07
FIRST OFFICER: Flaps.
CAPTAIN: They're at fifty [degrees].
FIRST OFFICER: Oh, Bill, I hope we can do it. I've got it, I got it. I'm going to land right over that guy.
CAPTAIN: There's a car ahead. . . .

1618:25

FIRST OFFICER: I got it, Bill, I've got it now, I got it.

CAPTAIN: Okay. Don't stall it. . . .

FIRST OFFICER: I gotta bug. We're going to do it right here.

1618:33

STEWARDESS ON   Bend down and grab your ankles.
  PA:

1618:34

FIRST OFFICER: I got it. (SOUND OF BREAKUP.)

1618:39

(MORE BREAKUP SOUNDS.)

1618:43

(SOUND OF IMPACT.)

Ingested water and hail had damaged the engine compressors of Flight 242, ultimately causing both engines to fail while the aircraft was cruising at 14,000 feet. When Flight 242 crashed, the fire that resulted destroyed a combination grocery store–gasoline station, a truck and five automobiles, along with numerous trees, shrubs, lawns, utility poles, power lines, mail boxes, highway signs, and fences. Although seriously injured, twenty-two of Flight 242's eighty-five passengers and crew survived the accident. The aircraft was destroyed.

2. United Airlines Flight 173 (UAL 173)

ON THAT AFTERNOON of 28 December 1978, the McDonnell-Douglas DC-8-61 of Flight 173 from JFK International Airport in New York to Portland International in Oregon required 31,900 pounds of fuel. With the 46,700 pounds the DC-8 carried that day, the Captain saw no reason for worry. At 1705:47, Flight 173 was making its approach to Runway 28. Flight 173 acknowledged, "We have the field in sight." Two seconds later, Flight 173 descended to 8,000 feet. The First Officer requested 15 degrees flaps and landing gear down. But the gear failed to lower.

"We got a [landing] gear problem," the Captain radioed. "We'll let you know."

Portland responded, "... Turn left, heading one zero zero and I'll just orbit you out there till you get your problem [solved]."

For the next twenty-three minutes, Flight 173 flew a holding pattern, while the flight crew discussed emergency procedures. At 1744:03, the Captain called the airline's Maintenance Control Center in San Francisco. He said, "I'm not going to hurry the girls. We got about a hundred seventy-five people [there were in fact one hundred eighty-one passengers on board] on board and we ... want to ... take our time and get everybody ready and then we'll go [in for an emergency landing]. It's clear as a bell and no problem."

The holding pattern kept Flight 173 at 5,000 feet and never more than twenty miles from the airport.

CAPTAIN (TO THE STEWARDESS WHO HAD COME INTO THE COCKPIT):	How you doing?

STEWARDESS:	We're ready for your announcement [to the passengers]. Do you have the signal for [when the passengers should assume] protective position? That's the only thing I need from you right now.
CAPTAIN:	Okay. Ah . . . what would you do? Have you got any suggestions about when to brace? Want to do it on the PA?
STEWARDESS:	I . . . I'll be honest with you. I've never had one of these [emergencies] before. My first, you know. . . .
CAPTAIN:	All right. What we'll do is we'll have Frostie [Second Officer] . . . oh, about a couple of minutes before touchdown signal for brace pattern.
PORTLAND:	173 heavy, turn left, heading two two zero.
FIRST OFFICER:	Left two two zero. . . .
STEWARDESS:	Okay.
CAPTAIN:	And then, ah . . .
STEWARDESS:	And if you don't want us to evacuate, what are you gonna say?
CAPTAIN:	We'll either use the PA or we'll stand in the door and holler.
STEWARDESS:	Okay, one or the other. Ah, we're reseating passengers right now, and all the cabin lights are full up.

1746:52

FIRST OFFICER:	How much fuel we got, Frostie?
SECOND OFFICER:	Five thousand [pounds].
AN OFF-DUTY CAPTAIN WHO COMES TO THE COCKPIT:	Less than three weeks, three weeks to retirement. You better get me outta here [safely].
CAPTAIN:	Thing to remember is, don't worry.
OFF-DUTY CAPTAIN:	What?
CAPTAIN:	Thing to remember is, don't worry.
OFF-DUTY CAPTAIN:	Yeah. . . . If I might make a suggestion. You should put your coats on, both for your protection and so you'll be noticed, so they'll [the passengers] know who you are.
CAPTAIN:	Oh, that's okay.
OFF-DUTY CAPTAIN:	But if it gets . . . if it gets hot, it sure is nice not to have bare arms.

CAPTAIN:	Yeah. . . . But if anything goes wrong, you just charge back there and get your ass off [this airplane], okay?
OFF-DUTY CAPTAIN:	Yeah. . . . I told . . . I told the gal to put me where she wants me. I think she wants me at a wing exit.
CAPTAIN:	Okay, fine. Thank you.
FIRST OFFICER:	What's the fuel show now, Buddy?
CAPTAIN:	Five [thousand pounds].

The Captain decided to remain in the holding pattern another fifteen minutes to burn off fuel, from 5,000 pounds down to slightly more than 3,000 pounds.

1751:09

FIRST OFFICER:	Maintenance have anything to say?
SECOND OFFICER:	He says, ''I think you guys have done everything you can,'' and I said we're reluctant to recycle the landing gear for fear something is bent or broken, and we won't be able to get [the gear] down.
FIRST OFFICER:	I agree.
CAPTAIN:	Ah, call the ramp, and give 'em our passenger count. . . . Tell 'em we'll land with about four thousand pounds of fuel and tell them to give that to the fire department. I want mechanics to check the airplane after we stop . . . before we taxi [to the gate].
SECOND OFFICER:	Yes, sir. [Then on the radio to Portland]: Flight 173, we will be landing, ah . . . in . . . ah, a little bit, and the information I'd like for you to pass on to the fire department for us. We have souls on board one seven two—one hundred and seventy-two, plus five ba . . . ah, lap . . . ah, children.
PORTLAND:	Okay, thank you.
SECOND OFFICER:	That would be five infants, that's one seven two, plus five infants . . . and we'll be landing with about three thousand pounds fuel and . . . ah, requesting as soon as we stop that mechanics meet the airplane for an inspection prior to taxiing further. . . .

1755:51

SECOND OFFICER:	Wind is three four zero at eight.

CAPTAIN:	Okay. . . . You want to be sure the flight bags and all that stuff is stowed and fastened down.
FIRST OFFICER:	How much fuel you got now?
SECOND OFFICER:	Four . . . four thousand . . . pounds.
FIRST OFFICER:	Okay.
CAPTAIN (TO SEC-OND OFFICER):	You might . . . you might just take a walk back through the cabin and kind of see how things are going. Okay? I don't want to . . . I don't want to hurry 'em, but I'd like to do it [attempt an emergency landing] in another . . . oh, ten minutes or so. . . . (THE SECOND OFFICER LEAVES THE COCKPIT.)
FIRST OFFICER:	If we do indeed have to evacuate, assuming that none of us are incapacitated, you're going to take care of the [engine] shutdown, right? Parking brakes, spoilers and flaps, fuel shut-off levels, fire handles, battery switch and all that?
CAPTAIN:	You just haul your ass back there and do whatever needs doing. I think that [stewardess] Jones is a pretty level gal . . . and sounds like she knows what she's doing, and Duke [the Off-Duty Captain] has been around for a while. I'm sure Duke will help out.
FIRST OFFICER:	We're not going to have any anti-skid protection, either.
CAPTAIN:	Well, I think the anti-skid is working. It's just the [indicator] lights ain't working. . . . I won't use much braking. We'll just let it roll out easy.
FIRST OFFICER:	You plan to land as slow as you can? With the power on?
CAPTAIN:	. . . I'm tempted to turn off the automatic spoilers to keep [the nose] from pitching down. . . .
SECOND OFFICER (RETURNS TO COCKPIT):	You've got another two or three minutes [to landing].
CAPTAIN:	How are the people?
SECOND OFFICER:	Well, they're pretty calm and cool and, ah . . . some of 'em are obviously nervous . . . ah, but for the most part, they're taking it in stride. I stopped and reassured a couple of them. They seemed a little bit more anxious than some of the others.
CAPTAIN:	Okay. Well, about two minutes before landing—that will be about four miles out [from the end of the runway]—just pick up the mike and say, "Assume the brace position."

SECOND OFFICER:	Okay. We got about three [thousand pounds] on the fuel, and that's it.
CAPTAIN:	Okay. On touchdown, if the gear folds or something really jumps the track, get those boost pumps off so that . . . you might even get the valves open.
PORTLAND CONTROL:	Flight 173, did you figure anything out yet about how much longer [to emergency landing]?
FIRST OFFICER:	Yeah. We . . . ah, have indication our [landing] gear is abnormal. It'll be our intention in about five minutes to land on 28 Left. We would like the equipment standing by. . . . We've got our people prepared for an evacuation in the event that should become necessary.
PORTLAND CONTROL:	173, okay. Advise when you'd like to begin your approach.
CAPTAIN:	Very well, They've about finished in the cabin. I'd guess about another three, four, five minutes.
PORTLAND CONTROL:	173, if you could . . . ah, give me souls on board and amount of fuel.
CAPTAIN:	One seven two passengers and about four thousand [pounds] . . . well, make it three thousand pounds of fuel.
SECOND OFFICER:	Plus six laps [infants].

1806:19

CAPTAIN (TO STEWARDESS WHO ENTERS THE COCKPIT):	How're you doing?
STEWARDESS:	Well, I think we're ready.
CAPTAIN:	Okay.
STEWARDESS:	We have . . . they have told me they've got able-bodied men by the windows. The Captain's [position after landing] in the very first row of coach after the galley. . . .
FIRST OFFICER:	Any invalids [among the passengers]?

1806:34

CAPTAIN:	Okay, we're going to go in [to land now]. We should be landing in about five minutes.
FIRST OFFICER:	I think you just lost Number Four [engine], Buddy. You . . .
STEWARDESS:	Okay, I'll make the five-minute announcement.

FIRST OFFICER:	Better get some cross feeds open [to engine Number Four], or something. . . .
STEWARDESS:	All righty.
FIRST OFFICER (ALARMED):	We're going to lose an engine, Buddy.
CAPTAIN:	Why?
FIRST OFFICER:	We're losing an engine.
CAPTAIN:	Why?
FIRST OFFICER:	Fuel! Open the cross feeds, man.
CAPTAIN:	Open the cross feeds or something.
SECOND OFFICER:	Showing fumes [only remained in the tank].
CAPTAIN:	Showing [on the gauges] a thousand [pounds of fuel] or better.
FIRST OFFICER:	I don't think it's in there.
SECOND OFICER:	Showing three thousand, isn't it?
CAPTAIN:	Okay. It's . . . it's . . .
FIRST OFFICER:	. . . a flameout!
CAPTAIN (TO PORTLAND CONTROL):	173 would like clearance for an approach into 28 Left. Now!
SECOND OFFICER:	We're going to lose Number Three [engine] in a minute, too.
CAPTAIN:	Well . . .
SECOND OFFICER:	It's [the fuel gauge] showing *zero*.
CAPTAIN:	You got three thousand pounds. . . . You got to . . .
SECOND OFFICER:	. . . [We're supposed to have] five thousand pounds of fuel in there, Buddy, but we lost it. . . .
CAPTAIN:	All right.
SECOND OFFICER:	Are you getting [reignition of the engine] back?
FIRST OFFICER:	No! You got that cross feed open?
SECOND OFFICER:	No, I haven't got it open. Which one . . . ?
CAPTAIN:	Open 'em both. God, get some fuel in there. Got some fuel pressure?
SECOND OFFICER:	Yes, sir.
THE CAPTAIN (TRYING TO START THE FUEL-STARVED ENGINE):	Rotation. Now she's coming. Okay. Watch [engines] One and Two. We're showing down to zero [on fuel] or a thousand [pounds].
SECOND OFFICER:	Yeah.

1808:11

FIRST OFFICER:	Still not getting it [the engine started].
CAPTAIN:	Well, open the cross feeds.
SECOND OFFICER:	All four [cross feeds]?
CAPTAIN:	Yeah.
FIRST OFFICER:	All right, now. It's coming. It's going to be a bastard on approach [to the airfield], though.
CAPTAIN:	Yeah. You gotta keep 'em [the engines] running, Frostie.
SECOND OFFICER:	Yes, sir.
FIRST OFFICER:	Get this mother on the ground.
SECOND OFFICER:	Yeah. It's not showing very much more fuel. . .
CAPTAIN (TO PORTLAND CONTROL):	173 has got the field in sight now. . . .
PORTLAND CONTROL:	Okay, 173. Maintain five thousand [feet].
CAPTAIN:	Maintain five.
SECOND OFFICER:	We're down to one [thousand pounds]. . . . Number Two [tank] is empty.
CAPTAIN (TO PORTLAND CONTROL):	173 is going to turn toward the airport and come on in.
PORTLAND CONTROL:	Okay. Now, you want to do it on a visual. Is that what you want?
CAPTAIN:	Yeah.
PORTLAND CONTROL:	Okay, 173. Turn . . . ah, left, heading three six zero and verify you do have the airport in sight.
FIRST OFFICER:	We do have the airport in sight.
PORTLAND CONTROL:	173 is cleared visual approach, Runway 28 Left.
FIRST OFFICER:	Cleared visual, 28 Left.
CAPTAIN:	Yeah.
	(THE SOUND OF THE ENGINES STILL OPERATING BEING REDUCED IN SPEED.)
FIRST OFFICER:	You want the Instrument Landing System on, Buddy?
CAPTAIN:	Well . . .
FIRST OFFICER:	It's not going to do any good now.
CAPTAIN:	No, we'll get that damned warning thing if we do.

1810:17

CAPTAIN:	Ah, reset that circuit breaker momentarily. See if we get [landing] gear [indicator] lights.

1810:24

CAPTAIN:	Yeah, the nose gear's down. About time to give that brace position [announcement to the passengers].
SECOND OFFICER:	Yes, sir.
CAPTAIN (TO PORTLAND CONTROL):	How far you show us from the field?
PORTLAND CONTROL:	Ah, I'd call it eighteen flying miles.
CAPTAIN:	All right.
SECOND OFFICER:	Boy, that fuel sure went to hell all of a sudden. I told you we had four [thousand pounds].

1811:14

CAPTAIN:	There's . . . ah, kind of an interstate highway-type thing along that bank on the river—in case we're short [of the runway].

1812:22

FIRST OFFICER:	Let's take the shortest route to the airport.
CAPTAIN (TO PORTLAND CONTROL):	What's our distance now?
PORTLAND CONTROL:	Twelve flying miles.
CAPTAIN (TO CREW):	About three minutes.
SECOND OFFICER:	We've lost two engines, guys!
FIRST OFFICER:	Sir?
SECOND OFFICER:	We just lost two engines—One and Two!
FIRST OFFICER:	You got all the pumps and everything?
PORTLAND CONTROL:	. . . You're about eight or niner flying miles from the airport.
SECOND OFFICER:	Yep.
PORTLAND CONTROL:	Have a good one.

1813:38

CAPTAIN:	They're all going! We can't make it!
FIRST OFFICER:	We can't make anything.
CAPTAIN:	Okay, declare a Mayday.

FIRST OFFICER **(TO PORTLAND** **CONTROL):**	173, *Mayday!* We're . . . the engines are flaming out. We're going down. We're not going to be able to make the airport!

1814:55

(SHOUTING IN THE COCKPIT AND THE SOUNDS OF THE IMPACT AS UNITED 173 HIT ELECTRICAL TRANSMISSION LINES.)

(SOUND OF IMPACT.)

United 173 crashed six miles from the airport. There was no fire. Of the 181 passengers and 8 crew members aboard, 8 passengers, the Second Officer, and a stewardess lost their lives. The aircraft was destroyed.

3. Air Florida Flight 90 (AFL 90)

ON 13 JANUARY 1982, a Boeing 737-222 of Air Florida pulled back from its gate at Washington, D.C.'s National Airport, with a scheduled destination of Fort Lauderdale. It was around 1530, snow was falling, and ice built up on the wings of the aircraft. Aboard Air Florida 90 that afternoon were seventy-seven passengers and five crew members.

1533:40

FIRST OFFICER: It's twenty-five [degrees outside]. It's not too cold really.

CAPTAIN: It's not really that cold.

FIRST OFFICER: It's not that cold—cold, like ten with the wind blowing, you know.

1534:24

CAPTAIN: Here comes the chain tractor [to pull their aircraft back from the gate.]

1535:40

FIRST OFFICER: I guess [I] never even thought about it being a little plane like this, figured they'd push it out of there, you know. But we're pretty heavy. We're a hundred and two thousand [pounds] sittin' there.

1536:13

FIRST OFFICER: Maybe we can taxi up 'side a some seven two sittin' there runnin', blow off whatever [accumulated on the wings].

1536:19

TRACTOR OPERATOR: You can start engines if you want. I don't know whether you got 'em running or not.

1536:50

CAPTAIN:	Checklist again, right?
FIRST OFFICER:	We did it and we're down to before start, that's all. Shoulder harness . . .
CAPTAIN:	On.
FIRST OFFICER:	Air-conditioning pack . . .
CAPTAIN:	Off.
FIRST OFFICER:	Start pressure. . . .
CAPTAIN:	Up.
FIRST OFFICER:	Anti-collision . . .
CAPTAIN:	On.
FIRST OFFICER:	Start's complete.

1537:01

FIRST OFFICER:	La Guardia's not accepting anybody right now.
STEWARDESS:	Is it raining in Tampa?
FIRST OFFICER:	Rainy and foggy.
STEWARDESS:	How is the temperature?
FIRST OFFICER:	Sixty [degrees].

1538:16

CAPTAIN:	After start . . .
FIRST OFFICER:	Electrical . . .
CAPTAIN:	Generators . . .
FIRST OFFICER:	Pilot heat . . .
CAPTAIN:	On.
FIRST OFFICER:	Anti-ice . . .
CAPTAIN:	Off.
FIRST OFFICER:	Air-conditioning pressurization . . .
CAPTAIN:	Packs on flight.
FIRST OFFICER:	Start levers . . .
CAPTAIN:	Idle.
FIRST OFFICER:	Door warning lights . . .
CAPTAIN:	Out.

1539:29

FIRST OFFICER:	Boy, this is shitty. It's probably the shittiest snow I've seen.

1540:15

CAPTAIN: . . . Go over to the hanger and get de-iced. . . .

FIRST OFFICER: Yeah. Definitely. It's been awhile since we've been de-iced.

1541:24

FIRST OFFICER: That [jet] over there. That guy's about ankle deep in it.

(SOUND OF LAUGHTER.)

1541:47

FIRST OFFICER: Hello, Donna.

STEWARDESS: I love it out here.

FIRST OFFICER: It's fun.

STEWARDESS: I love it. The neat way the tire tracks . . .

FIRST OFFICER: See that [jet] over there, looks like he's up to his knees . . .

STEWARDESS: Look at all the tire tracks in the snow.

1543:22

STEWARDESS: What does the *N* stand for on all the aircraft, before the number?

CAPTAIN: U.S. registered.

FIRST OFFICER: U.S. United States. See, every one of them have an *N* on it. See? Then you see somebody else like, ah.

1543:37

CAPTAIN: *C* is Canada, yeah, I think, or is it *Y*?

FIRST OFFICER: I think, I think it is *C*. There's, ah, you know, Venezuela. Next time you have a weird one, you can look up. Stand by a second.

1546:21

CAPTAIN: Tell you what, my windshield will be de-iced. Don't know about my wing.

1546:27

FIRST OFFICER: Well, all we really need is the inside of the wings anyway. The wing tips are gonna speed up by eighty anyway. They'll, they'll shuck all that other stuff.
(SOUND OF LAUGHTER.)

1547:32

CAPTAIN: [Gonna] get your wing now [with de-icing glycol].

1547:37

FIRST OFFICER: D' they get yours? Can you see your wing tip over 'er?

CAPTAIN: I got a little [ice] on mine.

FIRST OFFICER: A little. This one's got about a quarter to half an inch [of ice] on it all the way.

1548:24

FIRST OFFICER: See all those icicles on the back there and everything?

CAPTAIN: Yeah.

1548:59

FIRST OFFICER: See this difference in that left engine and right one.

CAPTAIN: Yeah.

FIRST OFFICER: Don't know why that's different. 'Less it's his hot air going into that right one. That must be it. From his exhaust. It was doing that in the chocks awhile ago, but, ah.

1549:32

GROUND CONTROL: Okay. Palm 90, cross Runway 3 and if there's space, then monitor the tower on nineteen one. Don't call him, he'll call you.

1550:08

FIRST OFFICER: I'm certainly glad there's people taxiing on the same place I want to go 'cause I can't see the taxiway without these flags.

1550:38

CAPTAIN: Where would I be if I were a holding line?

FIRST OFFICER: I would think that would be about right here, agreed? Maybe a little further up there. I don't know.

1551:23

STEWARDESS: We still fourth [in line for takeoff]?

FIRST OFFICER: Yeah.

STEWARDESS: Fourth now.

1551:38

FIRST OFFICER: We're getting there. We used to be seventh [in line].

1553:21

FIRST OFFICER: Boy, this is a, this is a losing battle here on trying to de-ice those things. It [gives] you a false feeling of security, that's all that does.

CAPTAIN: That, ah, satisfies the Feds.

FIRST OFFICER: Yeah. As good and crisp as the air is and no heavier than we are I'd . . .

CAPTAIN: Right there is where the icing truck, they oughta have two of them, you pull right . . .

FIRST OFFICER: . . . Right out . . .

CAPTAIN: . . . Like cattle, like cows right in between these things and then . . .

FIRST OFFICER: . . . Get your position back.

CAPTAIN: Now, you're cleared for takeoff. . . .

FIRST OFFICER: . . . Yeah and you taxi through kinda like a car wash or something. . . .

CAPTAIN: . . . Yeah. . . . Hit that thing with about eight billion gallons of glycol [de-icing liquid]. In Minneapolis, the truck they were de-icing us with, the heater didn't work on it, the glycol was freezing the moment it hit.

FIRST OFFICER: Especially that cold metal like that [on the wings].

CAPTAIN: Yeah. . . .

FIRST OFFICER: Boy, I'll bet all the school kids are just peeing in their pants here. It's fun for them, no school tomorrow, ya hoo! (SOUND OF LAUGHTER.)

1555:00

CAPTAIN: What do you think we should use for a takeoff alternative?

FIRST OFFICER: Well, it must be within an hour, is that Stewart up there within an hour? About thirty-five minutes up there, isn't it, on one. Dulles got a big old runway over there, probably about the same, probably about the same stuff as here, you know.

1555:36

CAPTAIN: Been into Stewart?

FIRST OFFICER: No, I've overflown it several times, over by the water over there, kinda long, it looks like an air force base, use'ta be something.

CAPTAIN:	Yeah. . . .
FIRST OFFICER:	Looks pretty good.

1555:44

CAPTAIN:	Yeah, it's a nice airport.

1556:39

TOWER:	Eastern 133 cleared for takeoff.
CAPTAIN:	Sure glad I'm not taking off in that piece of shit.

1556:42

EASTERN 133:	Cleared to go, Eastern 133's on the roll.

1556:43

FIRST OFFICER:	Yeah, that thing, right there, that gets your attention. Hopefully, that's, ah, is that turbo charged or fuel injected? Hate to blast outta here with carburetor ice all over me, 'specially with the [Washington] Monument staring you in the face.

1557:42

FIRST OFFICER:	Do you want to run everything but the flaps?
CAPTAIN:	Yeah.
FIRST OFFICER:	Start switches . . .
CAPTAIN:	They're on. Recall . . . checked . . . checked.

1557:48

FIRST OFFICER:	Flight controls . . .
CAPTAIN:	Bottom [of the wings].

1557:49

FIRST OFFICER:	Tops [of the wings] good. Let's check these tops again, since we've been setting here awhile. I think we get to go here in a minute. . . . Ought to work. Flaps we don't have yet. Stab [stabilizer] trim set at five point three.

1558:02

CAPTAIN:	Set.

1558:03

FIRST OFFICER:	Zero fuel weight, we corrected that up. Indicated airspeed bugs are a thirty-eight, forty, forty-four.

1558:20

CAPTAIN:	Set.

1558:21
FIRST OFFICER: Cockpit door . . .

1558:22
CAPTAIN: Locked.

1558:23
FIRST OFFICER: Takeoff briefing. Air Florida standard. Slushy runway. Do you want me to do anything special for this or just go for it?

1558:31
CAPTAIN: Unless you got anything special you'd like to do . . .

1558:33
FIRST OFFICER: Unless just takeoff the nose wheel early like a soft field takeoff or something. I'll take the nose wheel off [the ground] and then we'll let it fly off. Be out the three two six, climbing to five, I'll pull it back to about one point five five, supposed to be about one six, depending on how scared we are. (SOUND OF LAUGHTER.)

1559:06
CAPTAIN (ON PA): Ladies and gentlemen, we have just been cleared on the runway for takeoff, flight attendants please be seated.

1559:15
FIRST OFFICER: Flight attendant alert.

1559:16
CAPTAIN: Given.
FIRST OFFICER: Bleeds?

1559:17
CAPTAIN: They're off.

1559:18
FIRST OFFICER: Strobes, external lights . . .
CAPTAIN: On.

1559:19
FIRST OFFICER: Anti-skid . . .
CAPTAIN: On.

1559:21
FIRST OFFICER: Transponder . . .
CAPTAIN: On.

1559:24
TOWER: Palm 90 cleared for takeoff.

1559:28
TOWER: No delay on departure if you will. Traffic's two and a half out for the runway.

1559:32
CAPTAIN: Okay. Your throttles.

1559:46
FIRST OFFICER: Okay.

1559:48
(SOUND OF ENGINE SPOOL-UP.)

1559:49
CAPTAIN: Holler if you need the [windshield] wipers. It's spooled. Real cold, real cold.

1559:58
FIRST OFFICER: God, look at that thing! That don't seem right, does it? Ah, that's not right.

1600:09
CAPTAIN: Yes, it is, there's eighty [knots].

1600:10
FIRST OFFICER: Naw, I don't think that's right. Ah, maybe it is. . . .

1600:21
CAPTAIN: Hundred and twenty [knots].

1600:23
FIRST OFFICER: I don't know.

1600:31
CAPTAIN: Vee-One [takeoff decision speed]. Easy. Vee-Two [climb speed].

1600:39
(SOUND OF STICKSHAKER WARNING OF AN IMPENDING STALL.)

1600:41
TOWER: Palm 90, contact Departure Control.

1600:45
CAPTAIN: Forward, forward. Easy. We only want five hundred [feet]. Come on, forward. . . . Forward. Just barely climb.

1600:59
CAPTAIN: [Stalling] we're [falling].

1601:00
FIRST OFFICER: Larry, we're going down, Larry. . . .

1601:01
CAPTAIN: I know it.

(SOUND OF IMPACT.)

Following its takeoff from Runway 36 of National Airport, Air Florida 90 crashed into the barrier wall of the northbound span of the Fourteenth Street Bridge between the District of Columbia and Arlington County, Virginia, and plunged into the ice-covered Potomac River, finally coming to rest on the west side of the bridge, less than one nautical mile from the end of Runway 36. Four passengers and one crew member survived the crash.

4. Eastern Airlines Flight 855 (EAL 855)

MINUTES AFTER LEAVING Miami Airport bound for Nassau, the Bahamas, on 5 May 1983, while flying over water and executing a turn, EAL 855, a wide-bodied L-1011, flamed out in all three engines. The Cockpit Voice Recorder self-erased, but transmissions between Miami Center and EAL 855 were recorded. Aboard were 168 passengers and a crew of 10.

1318:16

MIAMI CENTER: Eastern 855, just continue on the heading. We'll have you back on radar shortly. Did you want any higher altitude?

EAL 855: Affirmative. We'd like to go up, ah . . . say, ah, oh, nineteen to twenty-one thousand [feet].

MIAMI CENTER: Okay, Eastern 855. Ah, what are you in, a left turn now?

1318:36

MIAMI CENTER: Eastern 855, climb to flight level two zero for now.

EAL 855: Twenty thousand, roger.

1319:43

MIAMI CENTER: Okay, 855, I have you back in radar here, leaving about one three six. . . . Proceed on two seven zero heading . . . radar vectors towards Biscayne.

EAL 855: Okay, two seven zero, heading back to, ah, Biscayne, roger.

1319:55

MIAMI CENTER: And any problem that we should know about?

EAL 855: We've, ah, we've had precautionary shutdown on Number Two engine.

1320:08

MIAMI CENTER: Okay, you need any special handling?

EAL 855: Negative, sir.

1320:12

MIAMI CENTER: Okay.

EAL 855: And Miami Center, Eastern, ah, 855, ah, we have, ah, some rather serious indications of all three oil pressures on all three engines, ah, ah, down to zero. We believe it to be faulty indications, ah, since the chances of all three engines having zero oil pressure and zero quantity is almost nil. However, that is our indication in the cockpit at the present time.

1323:46

MIAMI CENTER: Okay, fine. Why don't you turn right about fifteen degrees. We'll give you direct to Miami. Maintain flight level twenty thousand, whatever altitude you wanna maintain and we're just gonna have the [emergency] equipment standing by anyway for ya.

EAL 855: Miami Airport, roger, sir.

1324:27

MIAMI CENTER: And Eastern 855, giving you direct the Miami altimeter two nine zero four. We just need to know how many people you got on board.

EAL 855: Okay, sir, stand by one. One hundred and sixty-eight.

1324:54

MIAMI CENTER: One six eight, okay. Does that include your crew?

EAL 855: Negative, sir, ah, stand by on the crew.

1326:26

MIAMI CENTER: And did you find that crew amount yet there Eastern 855? Eastern 855, contact me on frequency one two seven zero, one twenty-seven zero. Eastern 855, you read okay?

EAL 855: And we're with ya.

1327:04

MIAMI CENTER: Okay, sir, would you contact me frequency one two, ah, seven point zero?

EAL 855: Sir, we're on twenty-seven zero right now.

1327:13

MIAMI CENTER: Okay, very good. . . . Eastern 855, how many crew members you have on board?

EAL 855: Well, we've got three in the cockpit. We'll have to count in the back and we'll give that to you in just a minute, sir.

1327:33

MIAMI CENTER: Okay.

EAL 855: We have seven [crew members] in the back.

1327:53

MIAMI CENTER: Seven in the back, okay. Eastern 855, you can descend and maintain twelve, one-two, thousand at your discretion.

1329:00

EAL 855: Ah, [this is] Eastern numba, Eastern 855. We've just lost our Number Two engine, sir.

1329:05

MIAMI CENTER: Okay, losing Number Two. You still got two turning?

EAL 855: Negative. We only have one now and, ah, we're gonna restart our Number Two engine.

1329:15

MIAMI CENTER: Okay, fine. We're listening. Okay, cleared direct Miami's altimeter two nine eight nine and you can descend at your discretion at any altitude you need. You're clear of traffic.

EAL 855: Okay. We need a heading, ah, we'd like a heading to go from, ah [runway] Left.

1329:57

MIAMI CENTER: Okay, your position right now is seventy miles southwest of Miami. You're about fourteen minutes out heading two eight five, two eighty-five, for Miami.

EAL 855: Two eighty-five, okay.

1330:07

MIAMI CENTER: And you can plan a straight-in [on Runway] 27 Left. We're telling Approach about it right now. Equipment will be standing by.

EAL 855: Roger.

1330:16

MIAMI CENTER: And if you're not busy, if you can, we need [a reading of the] fuel on board.

EAL 855: Say again, sir.

1330:22

MIAMI CENTER: If you're not busy, we need fuel on board.

EAL 855: Okay, we have, a thirty-six thou . . .

1330:28

MIAMI CENTER: Roger. Eastern 855, you're cleared to six [thousand feet] or any altitude you need. Advise. . . .

EAL 855: We'll advise. . . .

1331:15

MIAMI CENTER: Roger.

EAL 855: The wind at Miami please?

1332:26

MIAMI CENTER: And Eastern 855, if you can, can you give me a status report how you're doing?

EAL 855: We're doing okay.

1332:34

MIAMI CENTER: Okay. Eastern 855 your position now fifty-nine miles southwest of Miami Airport. Turn left about five degrees. You're about thirteen minutes out at your speed.

EAL 855: Roger.

1333:24

EAL 855: We're losing another engine. We've lost our third engine right now!

1333:40

MIAMI CENTER: Okay, have you got the other one started?

EAL 855: Not yet.

1333:44

MIAMI CENTER: Do you have any of them turning?

EAL 855: Negative.

1333:51

MIAMI CENTER: Just advise. The Coast Guard is coming out towards you now.

EAL 855: Roger.

1333:55

MIAMI CENTER: Keep me advised of your intentions and we'll keep you on here as long as we can. Approach is also watching you at the same time. You're about twenty miles west of Bimini right now. And it looks like you're gonna have to ditch; just keep us advised. We should be able to hear you at least down to twenty-five hundred feet.

EAL 855:   Yeah.

1335:23

MIAMI CENTER: Eastern 855 you're forty-nine miles southeast, southeast, of Miami right now, twelve minutes out at your speed.

EAL 855:   Okay, we don't believe we can make land, ah. . . .

1335:38

MIAMI CENTER: Okay, we've got all the help we can coming out as fast as we can.

1335:41

OPA-LOCKA COAST GUARD'S FALCON JET: We're a Falcon Jet coming off the beach at, ah, flying out of Opa-locka, ah, what's your position, sir?

1335:47

MIAMI CENTER: Okay, I'll tell you what. Coast Guard just give me an ident. I'll give you a position relation to yourself [unintelligible] code you squawking.

1335:53

COAST GUARD: Squawking one two seven seven.

1335:59

MIAMI CENTER: Okay, squawk ident. Okay, I see ya out there. He is one o'clock. Your position twenty miles. I'll vector you to him. I have you [in] radar contact.

1336:03

COAST GUARD: Roger, sir. Okay, we'll be turning to about a heading of one one zero [degrees].

1336:15

MIAMI CENTER: Okay, one one zero. Let's make it a one two zero [degrees]. We'll intercept closer.

1336:19
COAST GUARD: Roger, that one two zero. And, ah, what's his altitude?

1336:29
MIAMI CENTER: Right now seventy-nine hundred [feet] and he's descending slowly.

1336:33
COAST GUARD: Roger, we're climbing through twenty-five hundred.

1336:35
MIAMI CENTER: Roger. Try heading one three five [degrees]. Coast Guard, one three five [degrees].

1336:43
COAST GUARD: One three five.

1337:02
MIAMI CENTER: He's [at] twelve o'clock, ten miles [away], Coast Guard.

1337:06
COAST GUARD: Roger that.

1337:09
MIAMI CENTER: Coast Guard's gonna be right next to you here pretty soon, Eastern 855.

1337:15
COAST GUARD: Okay, ah. Ah, say his altitude again, sir.

1337:19
MIAMI CENTER: Eastern is sixty-nine hundred [feet] descending.

1337:22
COAST GUARD: Roger, we're thirty-two hundred [feet] climbing.

1337:24
MIAMI CENTER: Ah, roger.
EAL 855: [Unintelligible] direct to closest land point, please.

1337:36
MIAMI CENTER: Okay, just as straight in is about the best you can do right now, Eastern 855, the way it looks here. Are you over land now Coast Guard?

1337:45
COAST GUARD: Ah, negative, sir. We're off shore about, ah, about fifteen miles, about ten miles, fifteen miles.

1337:52
MIAMI CENTER (TO COAST GUARD): Okay, Eastern is a ten eleven [L-1011], ah, turn further right another ten degrees. He's out there about twelve o'clock, be crossing left to right about seven miles.

1338:05
COAST GUARD: Roger, just for your information there's a small scud, ah, thin layer, at about, ah, oh, four thousand feet.

1338:12
MIAMI CENTER: Okay, suggest you stay down. He's at fifty-two hundred [feet] descending. 855, suggest a heading of about another twenty degrees to the right.

1338:29
COAST GUARD: [Unintelligible] we have him [in sight].

1338:33
MIAMI CENTER: Eastern's forty-seven hundred descending, Coast Guard. He's about eleven-thirty, four or five miles.

1338:39
COAST GUARD: Ah, we have him [in sight] at twelve-thirty, sir.

1338:41
MIAMI CENTER: Okay, twelve-thirty. Keep him in sight. I'm gonna stop talking. Advise Approach what you have to do.

1338:45
COAST GUARD: Ah, negative, sir. He just went into the clouds.

1338:47
MIAMI CENTER: Okay, he's forty-four hundred feet [unintelligible]. No traffic that I can see underneath you.

1338:54
COAST GUARD: Roger. that.

1338:56
MIAMI CENTER: Okay, I'll tell you what. If you want to turn to a heading of one eight zero now we'll bring you in behind heading one eight, make it one *nine* zero.

1339:01
COAST GUARD: Roger, one nine zero.

1339:05
MIAMI CENTER: He's at forty-one hundred [feet] descending. Turn right heading two hundred degrees, Coast Guard.

1339:14
COAST GUARD: Two zero zero.

EAL 855:   We have an engine going now and we believe we can make the airport.

1339:22
MIAMI CENTER: Okay, you say you have one of them turning, Eastern?

EAL 855:   That's affirmative.

1339:25
MIAMI CENTER: Okay, the Coast Guard's gonna come in behind ya. He's behind ya right now. Coast Guard 277, turn right heading two five zero [degrees].

1339:32
COAST GUARD: Two five zero, turning.

1339:34
MIAMI CENTER: Okay, you're almost what? What are your flight conditions now, Eastern 855?

EAL 855:   In the clear.

1339:38
MIAMI CENTER: Okay, Coast Guard, you should have him in sight out there [unintelligible]. You make your right turn about twelve o'clock a mile and a half.

1339:44
COAST GUARD: Roger, sir, we have him.

1339:45
MIAMI CENTER: Okay, I'm gonna stop talking, Eastern. You're cleared a straight-in, contact Approach if you can. Don't talk if you don't have to.

EAL 855:   Cleared for a straight-in. We want 27 Left. Ah, we [unintelligible], are we in about pretty good for that?

1339:59
MIAMI CENTER: Ah, just go on in. We're waiting for ya.

1340:02
COAST GUARD: And this is the Coast Guard. Ah, we've lost him in the scud again.

1340:06
MIAMI CENTER: Okay, you're coming in behind him, about a mile behind him. He's at three thousand [feet] now. He's gonna be 27 Left.

1340:12
COAST GUARD: Roger.

1340:27
MIAMI CENTER: Okay, Coast Guard, you have him in sight?

1340:30
COAST GUARD: Ah, negative, sir.

1340:32
MIAMI CENTER: Okay, turn right, heading, ah, three zero zero degrees. He's looking, he's picking away from you, he's doing about three thousand [feet].

1341:21
COAST GUARD: We don't see him.

1341:22
MIAMI CENTER: Okay. And he's holding two three zero knots. He's looking in pretty good shape.

1341:27
COAST GUARD: Okay, we're at two four zero [knots] now and we'll follow him all the way into the airport, if that's okay with you.

1341:32
MIAMI CENTER: Okay, we'll tell Approach you're gonna be right behind him. Change to one two six eight five, that's one twenty-six eighty-five. That's Miami Approach, and tell them you're behind the Eastern.

1341:39
COAST GUARD: Roger, we have a visual now.

1341:41
MIAMI CENTER: Okay, very good.

1342:47
EAL 855: Well, we believe we've got it made.

1342:51

MIAMI CENTER: Fantastic!

EAL 855:   Of course we're cleared to land?!

1344:20

MIAMI CENTER: [Miami's Approach Control, are] you working Eastern 855?

1344:24

APPROACH   No, we're not talking to him. That's okay. Just let
CONTROL: him land.

1344:26

MIAMI CENTER: Okay, here he comes.

1344:27

APPROACH   Okay.
CONTROL:

1344:49

MIAMI CENTER: Eastern 855, you need not acknowledge if you're still on the frequency ground one, ah, ground point nine.

EAL 855:   Okay, sir, sure thank you for your help.

1344:58

MIAMI CENTER: Certainly.

EAL 855 landed safely without injury to its 168 passengers and crew of 10. A maintenance crew had failed to replace oil seals in all three of the L-1011's engines, which, when starved of oil soon after takeoff, heated up and flamed out.

5. Air Canada Flight 797 (AC 797)

―――――――――――――――

On 2 June 1983, while flying north over Cincinnati en route from Dallas to Toronto, Air Canada Flight 797, a DC-9 with forty-one passengers and five crew members aboard, experienced an electrical fire in the left rear bathroom. The fire soon spread throughout the aircraft, making vision nearly impossible for the flight crew in the cockpit. Part of the drama was recorded on the Cockpit Voice Recorder. The FAA recorded transmissions between the Cincinnati Approach Control and Flight 797.

1902:40 GMT

STEWARDESS (TO THE CAPTAIN):	Excuse me, there's a fire in the washroom at the back. . . .
CAPTAIN:	Oh, yeah?
STEWARDESS:	They're still, well . . . they're just gonna go back now.
FIRST OFFICER:	Want me to go there?
CAPTAIN:	Yeah, go. [To the Steward who had just brought his meal]: Leave my, leave my, leave my dinner in the thing there for a minute.
STEWARD:	Okay.
STEWARDESS:	Can I buy you a drink 'cause there's something going on, drink or a shot?
CAPTAIN:	Ah, I wouldn't say that.
STEWARDESS:	Yeah, okay.
FIRST OFFICER:	You got all the [circuit] breakers pulled out?
CAPTAIN:	The breakers are all pulled, yeah.

1903:31

STEWARDESS:	Captain, is it okay to move everybody up as far forward as possible?

1904:07

FIRST OFFICER: Okay, I, ah—you don't have to do it now. I can't go back now. It's [the smoke is] too heavy. I think we'd better go down [to land].

1904:16

STEWARDESS: I got all the passengers seated up front. You don't have to worry. I think it's gonna be easing up.

1904:23

FIRST OFFICER: Okay, it's starting to clear now.

CAPTAIN: Okay. Take the, take the smoke mask.

FIRST OFFICER: You have control?

CAPTAIN: Take the goggles. I'll leave the mask on.

FIRST OFFICER: Okay.

1904:46

CAPTAIN: Okay, go back whenever you can but don't get yourself incapacitated.

FIRST OFFICER: No problem, no problem.

CAPTAIN: Okay.

1905:36

STEWARDESS: Captain, your First Officer wanted me to tell you that [the Steward] has put a big discharge of CO_2 in the washroom. It [the fire] seems to be subsiding, all right.

1906:09

CINCINNATI: Canada 797, Cincinnati Center, go ahead.

1906:12

CAPTAIN: Yeah, we've got an electrical problem here. We may be off communication shortly. Ah, stand by.

STEWARD: Getting much better, okay. I was able to discharge half of the CO_2 inside the washroom even though I could not see the source but it's definitely inside the lavatory.

1906:50

CAPTAIN: Yeah, it's from the toilet, it's from the toilet.

1906:52

STEWARD: CO_2, it was almost half a bottle and it [the fire's] now almost cleared.

1906:54

CAPTAIN: Okay, thank you.

1906:55

STEWARD: Okay, good luck. (SOUND OF CLOSING COCKPIT DOOR.)

FIRST OFFICER: Okay, you got it.

CAPTAIN: Yeah. Okay.

FIRST OFFICER: I don't like what's happening. I think we better go
                           down, okay?

CAPTAIN: Okay.

2006:41   [Cockpit Voice Recorder goes off.]

2310:48

AIR CANADA 797   We have a fire in wash, in the back washroom
  TO CINCINNATI   and it's, ah, we're filling' up, ah, filling up, ah,
  APPROACH   with smoke right now.
  CONTROL:

2310:56

CINCINNATI   Understand, sir, and say type of airplane, ah,
  APPROACH   number of people on board and amount of fuel.
  CONTROL:

2311:00

AC 797:   Okay, we'll copy that later. I don't have time now.

2311:03

CINCINNATI   All right, sir, when able turn right zero nine zero
  APPROACH   [degrees] vector . . . and maintain five thousand,
  CONTROL: Air Canada 797.

2311:09

AC 797:   Air Canada 797, right turn heading zero nine zero
                           [degrees].

2311:15

CINCINNATI   Air Canada has a fire in the rear washroom [of]
  APPROACH   the airplane.
  CONTROL (TO
  CINCINNATI
  LOCAL CON-
  TROL):

2311:20

CINCINNATI LOCAL   In the what room?
  CONTROL:

2311:21

CINCINNATI
APPROACH CON-
TROL:

In the washroom.

2311:22

CINCINNATI LOCAL
CONTROL:

In the washroom, okay.

2311:24

CINCINNATI
APPROACH CON-
TROL:

Airplane is filling up with smoke.

2311:25

CINCINNATI LOCAL
CONTROL:

Filling up with smoke, okay.

2311:26

CINCINNATI
APPROACH CON-
TROL:

Right. Air Canada 797, stand by just a minute. Air Canada 797, if able squawk zero four zero five. Air Canada 797, can you make a right turn to zero nine zero [degrees]?

2312:44

AC 797:

Ah, what's the ceiling in, ah, Cincinnati?

2312:47

CINCINNATI
APPROACH CON-
TROL:

Two thousand five hundred feet scattered measured eight thousand feet over overcast, visibility one two miles with light rain. Air Canada 797, would you squawk zero four zero five and ident and say altitude?

2312:59

AC 797:

Zero four zero five. The altitude is, ah, eight thousand feet.

2313:10

CINCINNATI
APPROACH CON-
TROL:

Are you heading zero nine zero [degrees], Air Canada 797?

2313:13

AC 797:

Okay, we check, ah, we don't have any heading anymore, ah, all we have is, ah, a small horizon.

2313.22

CINCINNATI
APPROACH CON-
TROL:

Air Canada 797, say it again.

2313:24

AC 797:

We have no heading. We have no instrument, ah, all we have is a horizon right now.

2313.29

CINCINNATI
APPROACH CON-
TROL:

Can you give me a heading, ah, Air Canada 797?

2313:35

AC 797:

Stand by, we'll try.

2313:38

CINCINNATI
APPROACH CON-
TROL:

Air Canada 797, if able turn left. . . .

2313:41

AC 797:

Air Canada 797, turning left.

2314:03

CINCINNATI
APPROACH CON-
TROL:

Air Canada 797, this is a no-gyro surveillance approach for Runway 27 Left. Descend and maintain, ah, three thousand five hundred. Can you hold that altitude?

2314:13

AC 797:

Air Canada 797, that's affirmative.

2314:15

CINCINNATI
APPROACH CON-
TROL:

797, thank you. Stop turn. Your radar contact, your position is twelve miles southeast of Cincinnati Airport. A no-gyro surveillance approach to Runway 27 Left. You're cleared to land on that runway. The wind two two zero at four. Air Canada 797, the, ah, minimum descent altitude for Runway 27 Left one thousand two hundred eighty feet and, ah, the weather is, ah, good. . . . You should have no problem picking up the runway at that, ah, altitude.

2314:48

AC 797:

Canada 797, ah, we have no contact.

2314:51
CINCINNATI
APPROACH CON-
TROL:

Stop the traffic off the airport. Give me full approach lights for 27 Left. That's where he's comin' [in]. Air Canada 797, turn left.

2315:05
AC 797:

Air Canada 797, we're turning left.

2315:08
CINCINNATI
APPROACH CON-
TROL:

Air Canada 797, confirm altitude.

2315:11
AC 797:

Air Canada 797, ah, ah, twenty-five hundred feet.

2315:15
CINCINNATI
APPROACH CON-
TROL:

Air Canada 797, roger. You're fourteen miles southeast of the airport. Continue your left turn.

2315:20
AC 797:

Continue left turn. We don't see the airport. . . .

2315:23
CINCINNATI
APPROACH CON-
TROL:

Understand, sir. Advise me when you're VFR [Visual Flight Rules] conditions.

2315:27
AC 797:

We're VFR now. We do *not* see the airport.

2315:29
CINCINNATI
APPROACH CON-
TROL:

Understand. I'm turning you to the airport, Air Canada 797.

2315:44
CINCINNATI
APPROACH CON-
TROL:

Air Canada 797, stop your left turn.

2315:48
AC 797:

Air Canada 797 . . .

2315:52
CINCINNATI
APPROACH CON-
TROL:

Jean [name of local controller]?

2315:53

CINCINNATI LOCAL CONTROL: Yes?

2315:54

AC 797:   We have an airport at, ah, one o'clock. Is that it?

2315:58

CINCINNATI APPROACH CONTROL: Air Canada 797, ah, fly your present heading, sir. You might be looking at a satellite airport. I want to confirm it's Cincinnati, twelve-thirty and twelve miles.

2316:07

AC 797:   Air Canada 797, okay, we're maintaining two thousand.

2316.11

CINCINNATI APPROACH CONTROL: Air Canada 797, you are cleared to land on Runway 27 Left. The wind two three zero at four.

2316:16

AC 797:   Cleared to land. We don't see the runway.

2316:18

CINCINNATI APPROACH CONTROL: All right, sir, present heading is taking you to the field.

2316:34

CINCINNATI APPROACH CONTROL: Air Canada 797, turn left.

2316:37

AC 797:   Air Canada 797, turn left and, ah, we see obstruction [garbled].

2316:50

CINCINNATI APPROACH CONTROL: Air Canada 797, stop your left turn.

2316:54

AC 797:   Canada 797, where's the airport?

2316:56

CINCINNATI
APPROACH CON-
TROL:

Twelve o'clock and eight mil, ah, eight miles.

2317:02

AC 797:

Okay, we're trying [to] locate it. Advise, ah, people on the ground, ah, we're gonna need, ah, fire trucks.

2317:11

CINCINNATI
APPROACH CON-
TROL:

The trucks are standing by for you, Air Canada. Can you give me the number of people and amount of fuel?

2317:15

AC 797:

We don't have time. It's getting worse here. . . .

2317:16

CINCINNATI
APPROACH CON-
TROL:

Understand, sir, ah, turn left now and you're, ah, just a half a mile north of final approach course.

2317:22

AC 797:

Turning left.

2317:24

CINCINNATI
APPROACH CON-
TROL:

Give me full runway lights.

2317:25

CINCINNATI LOCAL
CONTROL:

Full runway lights.

2317:27

CINCINNATI
APPROACH CON-
TROL:

Air Canada 797, stop turn.

2317:30

AC 797:

Canada 797 . . . Okay, we have the airport [in sight].

2317:36

CINCINNATI
APPROACH CON-
TROL:

Air Canada 797, proceed inbound for 27 Left. You're cleared to land, wind two three zero at four. You're just a little bit north of the final approach course for Runway 27.

2317:48

AC 797:

Okay, it's a patch fire an' we're getting smoke.

2317:52

CINCINNATI APPROACH CONTROL:

You're gonna have to have the trucks come right up to him. He got, ah, smoke and fire on board.

2317:55

CINCINNATI LOCAL CONTROL:

Okay.

2317:59

CINCINNATI APPROACH CONTROL:

He does not have time to give me people or fuel.

2318:01

CINCINNATI LOCAL CONTROL:

Okay.

2318:10

CINCINNATI APPROACH CONTROL:

Air Canada 797, the equipment is waiting for you. You need not acknowledge further transmissions, ah, from me, Air Canada 797. You are cleared to land. You're four miles east of the airport.

2318:48

CINCINNATI APPROACH CONTROL:

Air Canada 797, you're on a three-mile final. Do you have him in sight?

2318:59

CINCINNATI LOCAL CONTROL:

Yes.

2319:01

CINCINNATI APPROACH CONTROL:

797, the tower has you in sight and you are cleared to land. You're on a two-mile final for 27 Left, the wind is two two zero at four.

2319:08

AC 797:

Air Canada 797, patch fire. Okay, get the truck.

2320:08

CINCINNATI APPROACH CONTROL:

Let me know when he lands, please.

2320:09

CINCINNATI LOCAL   He's landed.
  CONTROL:

2320:10

CINCINNATI   Okay.
  APPROACH CON-
  TROL:

Twenty-three passengers died in AC 797 as flames and noxious fumes, fanned by oxygen from opened emergency evacuation doors, filled the cabin after the Captain had brought the aircraft to a stop. Eighteen passengers and all five crew members survived. The aircraft was destroyed.

6. American Airlines Flight 96 (AA 96)

ON 12 JUNE 1972, American Airlines Flight 96, a DC-10-10, a scheduled passenger flight from Detroit to Buffalo, pulled back from the ramp at 0011. According to the Second Officer, the cargo door warning light on his panel in the cockpit never illuminated during the taxi-out or at any time during the flight to indicate that a cargo door had not been properly secured. There were fifty-six passengers aboard and a crew of eleven.

0018:47.5

CAPTAIN:	Are you ready, ah, Page [the First Officer], ah Page?
FIRST OFFICER:	Oh, thank you.
CAPTAIN:	Wanna try one [a takeoff]?
FIRST OFFICER:	All right, sir, thank you.
CAPTAIN:	I'll bring it up to a stop here [on the taxi ramp].
FIRST OFFICER:	Okay.
CAPTAIN:	It's still position-and-hold for us on the air.
SECOND OFFICER:	Okay we've got an anti-skid to go.

0019:14.0

LOCAL CONTROL:	American 96, maintain runway heading, contact Departure, cleared for takeoff.

0019:19.0

CAPTAIN:	American 96 is cleared for takeoff.
LOCAL CONTROL:	To maintain runway heading.
CAPTAIN:	To maintain runway heading. [To First Officer]: Okay, you can take it with the rudders.
FIRST OFFICER:	Okay. (SOUND OF ENGINE NOISE LEVEL INCREASES.)

CAPTAIN:	He [Local Control] said maintain heading.
FIRST OFFICER:	Yeah.
CAPTAIN:	Yeah. Okay, you got it.
FIRST OFFICER:	Okay.
CAPTAIN:	Get your hand on the wheel.
FIRST OFFICER:	I gotcha.

0019:48.0

CAPTAIN:	Vee-One . . . rotate
FIRST OFFICER:	. . . forward main gear up.

0020:11.5

LOCAL CONTROL:	American 96, maintain runway heading, contact Departure one eighteen four.
CAPTAIN:	One eighteen four maintain runway heading, American, ah, 96.
DEPARTURE RADAR:	American 96, Detroit Departure, radar contact climb and maintain six thousand.

0020:42.0

CAPTAIN:	Okay, you want us to climb and maintain six thousand, American, ah, 96.
DEPARTURE RADAR:	Roger, American 96, turn heading zero six zero.

0020:50.5

CAPTAIN:	Right to zero six zero, American 96. [To First Officer]: Okay, you got 'em?
FIRST OFFICER:	Yeah. Flaps, up. (SOUND OF FLAP LEVER.)

0021:23.0

DEPARTURE RADAR:	American 96, turn right heading zero nine zero.
CAPTAIN:	Right to zero nine zero, American 96. [To First Officer]: Zero nine zero, you got it?
FIRST OFFICER:	Slats up. (SOUND OF CLICK.)
CAPTAIN:	Whoever designed that thing, I'll tell yah, he— ooh . . .
FIRST OFFICER:	They're really something to behold, huh?
SECOND OFFICER:	Gear handle to . . . (SOUND OF CLICK.)

0022:15.0

DEPARTURE RADAR:	American 96, turn right heading one one zero, join, ah, Jay five five four when ya intercept.

CAPTAIN:	Okay, ah, take over on Victor ninety-four when we intercept, American 96, and, ah, six thousand still our altitude?

0022:33.0

DEPARTURE RADAR:	Okay, ah, I'll have something higher for ya here in just a moment and that'd be Vic Jay five five four to resume normal navigation on [pause]. Jay fifty-four to American 96, climb and maintain, ah, flight level two one zero. (SOUND OF WARNING HORN.)

0022:45.5

CAPTAIN:	Okay, ah, climb two one zero, American 96, we're out of, ah, fifty-five hundred now.

0022:54.0

DEPARTURE RADAR:	And would you verify, were you issued Jay five five four? I misunderstood you, I believe.

0022:58.5

CAPTAIN:	That is correct, ah, take over on five five four and inter—and, ah, flight plan route American, ah, 96.

0023:07.5

DEPARTURE RADAR:	American 96 can call Cleveland Center now on frequency one two six point four. Good day.

0023:07.5

CAPTAIN:	Call for 'em, Page, and I'll try to set 'em up for you, okay?
FIRST OFFICER:	Thank you.

0023:13.0

CAPTAIN:	Ah, repeat that frequency, I'm sorry.
DEPARTURE RADAR:	One two six point four. Twenty-six four, good day now.

0023:18.0

CAPTAIN:	Good day.
FIRST OFFICER:	[I can do this], but I'll be late.
CAPTAIN:	Okay, I expect you to do it when I'm a few minutes late.
FIRST OFFICER:	Thank you.

0023:37.0

CAPTAIN: Good evening, Cleveland Center, American Flight 96 is out of, ah, seven thousand now for two one zero.

0023:47.0

CLEVELAND CENTER: American 96 squawk code, ah, one one zero zero and ident, maintain flight level two three zero, report reaching.

0023:58.0

CAPTAIN: Okay, one one zero and ident and report reaching two one zero American 96.

FIRST OFFICER: Two three zero [23,000 feet].

0024:05.0

CAPTAIN: Ah, correction, was that two three zero?

CLEVELAND CENTER: Two three zero, American 96 reaching . . .

0024:10.5

CAPTAIN: Okay, American 96 . . .

CLEVELAND CENTER: Ninety . . .

0024:28.5

CAPTAIN: [There] goes a big one up there. (SOUND OF AMPLI-TUDE NOISE.) What the hell was it? (WHISTLE SIMILAR TO HUMAN VOICE; SOUND OF FIRE WARNING HORN BEGINS AT SAME TIME WITH ALTITUDE WARNING HORN.) We'll pass the warning fire.

FIRST OFFICER: Which one?

The crew in the cockpit had heard and felt a definite "thud." Dust and dirt had flown up in their faces, momentarily blinding the Captain, who thought that a midair collision had occurred and that the windshield had been lost. The rudder pedals had moved to the full left-rudder position, all three thrust throttle levers had moved back to near the flight-idle position, and the aircraft had yawed to the right. The Captain immediately had disengaged the autopilot and had taken the controls in his hands. Number One and Three engines responded, but the Captain could not move the Number Two thrust lever. The airspeed was stabilized at 250 knots. The Captain declared an emergency and Air Route Traffic Control cleared the flight back to Detroit.

0024:42.5

SECOND OFFICER: We've hit something.

FIRST OFFICER: We've lost . . . lost an engine here.

0024:46.5

CAPTAIN: Ah, which one is it?

FIRST OFFICER: Two.

SECOND OFFICER: Number One [engine] is still good. And, ah, Captain . . . we'll have to . . . to check this out.

FIRST OFFICER: Okay, apparently . . . master warning. This board's got an engine fire over here. Yeah, we got the engines, One and Three. Do we have, ah, hydraulics?

CAPTAIN: No! I've got full rudder here.

SECOND OFFICER: Hydraulic pressure's okay.

STEWARDESS: Is everything all right up here?

0025:16.5

CAPTAIN: No! Ah, Center, this is American Airlines 96, we got an emergency.

SECOND OFFICER (TO STEWARDESS): You go back to the . . .

0025:22.0

CLEVELAND CENTER: American 96, roger returning back to Metro.

0025:25.0

CAPTAIN: Ah, negative, I want to get into an airport that's in the open. Where's one open?

0025:29.0

CLEVELAND CENTER: American 96, start right turn, heading'll be one one seven zero, maintain one zero thousand, go ahead.

CAPTAIN: Right turn to one zero thousand?

0025:37.0

CLEVELAND CENTER: Right turn heading one eight zero, maintain ten thousand, go ahead. American 96, Cleveland.

0025:51.0

FIRST OFFICER: We got seven zero heading, sir, and, ah, maintaining twelve thousand.

0025:54.5
CLEVELAND
    CENTER:

Nine six roger, type of emergency?

FIRST OFFICER:

[Misunderstanding question]: Yeah, yes, sir.

CAPTAIN:

We have a control problem, we have no rudder, got full jam, we've had something happen, I don't know what it is.

0026:06.5
CLEVELAND
    CENTER:

American 96, understand . . . cleared to maintain, ah, niner thousand, altimeter two niner eight seven be, ah, radar vector back toward the ILS [Instrument Landing System] course Runway 3. You want the [emergency] equipment to be standing by?

0026:22.0
FIRST OFFICER:

Okay, sir, ah, ah, say again the heading and we'll let down slowly to niner thousand.

0027:21.0
CAPTAIN:

Okay, now, we've got, ah, problem. I got a hole in the cabin, I think we've lost Number Two engine, we've got a jammed rudder full left rudder and we need to, ah, get down and make an approach. I guess Detroit Metro would be the best and, ah, can you vector us around?

0027:42.5
CLEVELAND
    CENTER:

American 96, roger turn further right now, heading'll be two zero zero.

0028:25.0
CAPTAIN:

I have no rudder control whatsoever so our turns are gonna have to be very slow and cautious.

0028:31.0
CLEVELAND
    CENTER:

Understand.

0028:33.0
FIRST OFFICER:

Okay, we've got full control on this though, however, so I guess we're slow enough so we can probably use differential directions with engines. Thank goodness it's One and Two we've got . . . One and Three.

0028:54.0
CLEVELAND
  CENTER:

American 96, continue descent to five thousand feet. Say the altitude now.

0028:58.5
FIRST OFFICER:

Twelve thousand to five [thousand feet].

0029:57.0
CLEVELAND
  CENTER:

Nine six altitude now.

0029:58.5
FIRST OFFICER:

Ah, eleven thousand two hundred.

0031:12.5
CAPTAIN (TO FIRST
  OFFICER):

Okay. Give me about fifteen on the flaps now. Watch it carefully.

0032:06.0
SECOND OFFICER:

We'll be landing about two hundred ninety-two thousand [pounds].

0032:45.0
FIRST OFFICER:

We're out of eight seven hundred for, ah, five thousand right?

0032:48.5
CLEVELAND
  CENTER:

American 96, roger, turn back right now, heading'll be two eight zero. American 96 now cleared to maintain three thousand [feet].

0034:34.0
FIRST OFFICER:

Three thousand . . .

0035:13.0
CLEVELAND
  CENTER:

American 96, Metro Approach one two one five—one twenty-five fifteen go ahead.

0035:18.5
FIRST OFFICER:

Thank you, one twenty-five one five.

0036:08.5
FIRST OFFICER (TO
  CAPTAIN):

We've got a nice rate of descent; even if we have to touch down this way we're doing well.

0036:30.0
ARRIVAL RADAR:

American 96, Detroit.

0036:32.0
FIRST OFFICER: Loud and clear, sir, and we're through five thousand five hundred four three.

0036:45.5
ARRIVAL RADAR: American 96, turn right heading three six zero, descend and maintain three thousand, vector to the ILS 3 Left final approach course, altimeter two niner eight five, visibility one and one half, breaking, clear for all types of aircraft.

0036:57.0
FIRST OFFICER: I think you['re] heading now to three thousand.

0038:40.0
CAPTAIN (TO FIRST OFFICER): Well, gimme the [landing] gear. . . . Okay, here we're coming into the ILS. I'm gonna start slowing her down, give me twenty-two on the flaps. All right, we got the green lights.

0041:10.0
ARRIVAL RADAR: American 96, you're two and a half miles from the marker, contact the tower one two one point one, good night.

0041:15.0
FIRST OFFICER: Good night, sir.

0042:23.5
LOCAL CONTROL: American 96 cleared to land.

0042:26.5
FIRST OFFICER: American 96 cleared to land.

0042:42.0
CAPTAIN (TO FIRST OFFICER): Give me thirty-five on the flaps. I have no rudder to straighten it out with when it hits.

American 96 landed 1,900 feet down the runway and immediately started to veer to the right. The Captain applied reverse thrust to engines Number One and Three and applied full left aileron. As the aircraft veered farther right, the First Officer applied full reverse thrust to the left engine and brought the right engine out of reverse. The airplane ran parallel to the right side of the runway for 2,800 feet before gradually turning back left to the runway. The airplane stopped 8,800 feet from the runway threshold with the nose and left main landing gear off the runway surface.

The Captain ordered an emergency evacuation. All passengers and crew used the inflatable slides, to evacuate the aircraft. Two crew members and nine passengers were injured.

0044:53.5

FIRST OFFICER (AS PASSENGERS EVACUATED THE AIRCRAFT):

Okay, now engines off at your discretion.

0044:55.0

CAPTAIN:

Shut 'em down!

7. *Turkish Airlines Flight 981 (TA 981)*

On 3 March 1974, a Turkish Airline's DC-10 lifted off Orly's Runway 08 at just after 1230. Flight 981, carrying 346 passengers of 21 nationalities, headed due east, bound for Heathrow Airport, London. As air traffic regulations demanded, the flight path avoided overflying Paris. The takeoff was flawless and the climb-out smooth. Nothing during the first nine minutes of flight created any sense of alarm, especially at the Air Traffic Control Center at Orly. However, suddenly the dot that had represented Flight 981 on the radar screen disappeared without explanation.

At 12,500 feet the pressure differential inside the Turkish Airline's DC-10 had represented almost five tons of air pressing against the inside of a faulty rear cargo door. The latches on the faulty door gave way, and the door blew open, to be ripped from its hinges, just as it had done aboard AA 96 (see page 68). The DC-10 had decompressed rapidly. In that rush of decompression the cabin floor collapsed. The last two rows of seats in the left-hand aisle—and the six passengers in those seats—plunged into the hole of the caved-in floor and were blown out of the fuselage, falling two and a half miles to earth. When the floor collapsed, the control cables (hydraulics, in the terminology) running to the tail jammed or were severed. The crew in the cockpit of 981 had no means—not even the use of the throttles, as had the Captain of AA 96—to control the aircraft or prevent its nose from plunging below the horizon.

CAPTAIN: Oops. Aw. aw.

(A HORN SOUNDS A WARNING IN THE COCKPIT.) [There is violent decompression in the cockpit. Dust creates a dense mist. Nine seconds have passed since the decompression.]

FIRST OFFICER:	What happened?
CAPTAIN:	The cabin blew out.

[Eleven seconds have passed.]

FIRST OFFICER:	Are you sure?
CAPTAIN:	Bring it up! Pull her nose up!
FIRST OFFICER:	I can't bring it up. She doesn't respond.

[Sixteen seconds have passed.]

CAPTAIN:	*Acaba, nedir, nedir?* ["Wonder what it is, what it is. . . ."—the catchline from a popular Turkish TV commercial.]

[Twenty-three seconds have passed.]

SECOND OFFICER:	Nothing is left.
FIRST OFFICER:	Seven thousand feet.

(A HORN SOUNDS TO WARN THAT THE AIRPLANE HAS EXCEEDED THE "NEVER-EXCEED" SPEED.)

[Thirty-two seconds have passed.]

CAPTAIN:	Hydraulics?
FIRST OFFICER:	We have lost it. . . . Oops, oops!

[Fifty-four seconds have passed.]

CAPTAIN:	It looks like we are going to hit the ground.

[Fifty-six seconds have passed.]

(SOUND OF IMPACT.)

Flight 981 hit the ground at 490 miles per hour. None of the 346 passengers and crew survived. The aircraft was destroyed.

8. Pan American Clipper Flight 160 (PAA 160)

ON 3 NOVEMBER 1973, Pan American World Airways Clipper Flight 160, a Boeing 707-3210, was a scheduled cargo flight from JFK International Airport, New York, to Frankfurt, Germany, with a scheduled stop at Prestwick, Scotland. The flight departed JFK at 1325 Greenwich Mean Time with 52,912 pounds of cargo aboard, 15,360 pounds of which were chemicals. The flight crew consisted of a Captain, a First Officer, and a Flight Engineer. After departure, Pan Am 160 was vectored on a course while climbing to 33,000 feet. At 1404, one hundred miles out of Montreal, Canada, the Captain advised Pan Am Operations in New York that smoke had accumulated in the "Lower 41," an electrical compartment, and that the flight was diverting to land in Boston.

1404:24.5

CAPTAIN: Ah, yes sir, we have, ah, accumulation of smoke in the Lower Forty-one and we're gonna go back to Boston. Do you want us back in Boston or back in New York?

1404:34.0

PAN AM OPERA-
TIONS: Ah, stand by, 160, we'll find out.

1404:43.0

CAPTAIN (TO FIRST
OFFICER): New York is not that much further on so we can just go ahead back.

FIRST OFFICER: Do you think? Do you wanna go to New York?

CAPTAIN: I asked him where did he want us now.

1405:07.0

CAPTAIN: Dave?

SECOND OFFICER: Yeah?

1405:08.5

CAPTAIN: You don't think you could get down there and spot that [fire], huh?

SECOND OFFICER: I can't get around down there at all. I . . .

FIRST OFFICER: [Can] we increase our airflow so we can get rid of some of the smoke through the outflow valve[s] and equipment cooling [circuit]?

1405:38.0

CAPTAIN: Just stick your head down and see if [the smoke's] still coming.

FIRST OFFICER: I requested direct Boston radar vectors, but they haven't given me anything yet.

1405:49.5

CAPTAIN: Pan Op from the Clipper 160.

PAN AM OPERA-
TIONS: 160, go ahead.

CAPTAIN: Ah, did you get that message? Do you want us to come back to New York or go into Boston?

1405:59.5

PAN AM OPERA-
TIONS: . . . They're checking on that right now. Copied you've got an accumulation of smoke in your Lower Forty-one. They're, ah, finding out where they would like you. Ah, 160, they say come back to New York, and, ah, when you get a moment you can give us a good ETA [estimated time of arrival] for New York.

1406:17.0

CAPTAIN: Stand by. We'll just get our, ah, routing back to New York first.

FIRST OFFICER: Montreal Center, Clipper 160.

1408:45.0

MONTREAL CEN-
TER: Clipper 160, Montreal—squawk—ident say the altitude.

1408:48.5

FIRST OFFICER: Clipper 160, level at three one zero and we wanna go right back to Kennedy at this time.

MONTREAL
CENTER: Clipper 160, roger. Turn right heading one eight zero.

FIRST OFFICER: Right turn to one eight zero, thank you.

1409:19.5

CAPTAIN (TO SEC-OND OFFICER):	It's still getting thicker, isn't it?
SECOND OFFICER:	Seems like there could be equiprnent.
CAPTAIN:	There is no smoke in those smoke detectors though, is there?

1409:29.5

SECOND OFFICER:	Yes, there is now.
CAPTAIN:	There is?
SECOND OFFICER:	Yeah.

1409:58.0

SECOND OFFICER:	We oughta go on oxygen, this [is] getting a little thick, eh?
FIRST OFFICER:	I do too.
CAPTAIN:	Just wait till we—go ahead . . . Pan Ops from the Clipper 160.
PAN AM OPERA-TIONS:	160, Pan Op New York, go . . .
CAPTAIN:	Yes, sir, we just got our clearance to, ah—for a one eighty. We're coming back to New York and it seems to be getting a little thicker in here.
PAN AM OPERA-TIONS:	New York Clipper 160, understand that you're turning around now and returning to New York and the smoke is thicker. Ah, will you be requesting [emergency] equipment on arrival?

1410:27.0

MONTREAL CENTER:	Clipper 160, you're cleared to Kennedy direct—
CAPTAIN:	Ah, we'll let you know a little later on. I think we have a few minutes.
PAN AM OPERA-TIONS:	Very good, sir, thank you.
FIRST OFFICER:	Montreal, you were blocked out. Understand direct Kennedy and say the rest.
MONTREAL CENTER:	For now contact Boston one two eight seven five.

1410:45.0

FIRST OFFICER:	Roger, roger, direct Kennedy one twenty-eight seventy-five, good day.
SECOND OFFICER (TO CAPTAIN):	I think we better take it to Boston.

CAPTAIN:	Yeah.
SECOND OFFICER:	This [smoke] is getting thick back here.

1411:00.5

FIRST OFFICER:	New York, this is the Clipper 160.
CAPTAIN:	And tell 'em we wanna get down and head for Boston.
FIRST OFFICER:	Right.
PAN AM OPERA- TIONS:	Okay, go ahead.
FIRST OFFICER:	Yes, sir, I think we're gonna take this thing into Boston. This smoke is getting too thick.
PAN AM OPERA- TIONS:	Understand you're going to Boston [because] the smoke is too—stand by one . . .

1411:17.0

FIRST OFFICER:	Boston Center, Clipper 1 . . . (START OF OXYGEN MASK SOUND.)

1411:20.0

CAPTAIN:	Wait a minute. What . . . was that [Boston Center radio frequency] number?
FIRST OFFICER:	One twenty-eight seventy-five.
CAPTAIN:	You back on that one, okay.
FIRST OFFICER:	Descent check . . .

1411:33.0

FIRST OFFICER:	Boston Center, Clipper 160 requesting direct Boston and, ah, requesting descent.

1411:40.0

BOSTON CENTER:	Clipper 160, ah, roger, stand by just one sec— and, ah, wha—, how low would you like to go?

1411:46.0

FIRST OFFICER:	Ah, say again, please.
BOSTON CENTER:	160, Boston, are you in an emergency or anything?

1411:54.0

FIRST OFFICER:	Boston, please give me a landing direct Boston at this time.
BOSTON CENTER:	160, pick up a heading of, ah, one seven zero and when able, proceed direct to Boston.
FIRST OFFICER:	Thank you very much.

1412:07.0

CAPTAIN (TO BOSTON CENTER): Ah, we'd like to start our descent also if possible.

BOSTON CENTER: 160, descend and maintain flight level one eight zero, correction, one nine zero.

1412:14.0

PAN AM OPERATIONS: 160, Pan Op . . .

1412:16.0

CAPTAIN: Yes, sir, we're out of three one for one nine zero.

PAN AM OPERATIONS: 60—

1412:25.0

CAPTAIN (TO CREW): D'you guys want to get your goggles?

1412:28.0

SECOND OFFICER (TO PAN AM OPERATIONS): Pan Op go ahead.

PAN AM OPERATIONS: Are you requesting [emergency] equipment on arrival [at] Boston, sir?

1412:33.0

SECOND OFFICER (TO CAPTAIN): D'you want equipment on arrival at Boston? Probably wouldn't hurt, huh?

CAPTAIN: Stand by one, I don't—know—what did—how's the smoke doing?

1412:43.0

SECOND OFFICER: [It] is full back there. . . .

1412:48.0

CAPTAIN: Better have the equipment.

1412:52.0

SECOND OFFICER (TO PAN AM OPERATIONS): Okay, we want the equipment Boston, ah, cockpit's full back here.

PAN AM OPERATIONS: Okay, we're on the phone with them right now.

1412:57.5

FIRST OFFICER: Boston Center, Clipper 160 . . . Bost—Boston Center, Clipper 160.

1413:36.0

SECOND OFFICER: Okay, I'll give ya the descent check here, stand by. . . . Okay, radio altimeters . . . they're on.

1413:43.0

BOSTON CENTER: 160, Boston, would you say the nature of your problem please?

1413:47.0

FIRST OFFICER: The Clipper 160 is out of twenty-five point five.

SECOND OFFICER (TO CAPTAIN): Okay, fire warning. I'm gonna check the fire warning.

1413:51.0

CAPTAIN: Go ahead. (SOUND OF FIRE WARNING BELL.)

1413:53.0

BOSTON CENTER: 160, ah, Boston, roger, can you say again the, ah, nature of your emergency?

1413:58.0

FIRST OFFICER: Ah, we have smoke in the cockpit at this time.

1414:01.0

BOSTON CENTER: 160, roger.

1414:25.5

FIRST OFFICER: Boston Center, Clipper 160.

BOSTON CENTER: 160, Boston Center, ident.

FIRST OFFICER: Identing and, ah, please, ah, just keep me on this frequency. It's too hard to change.

BOSTON CENTER: Okay, I'll keep you on this frequency, roger, sir, fly direct Kennebunk.

1414:42.5

FIRST OFFICER: Kennebunk, ah . . .

BOSTON CENTER: And, ah, understand you have smoke in the cockpit, sir.

FIRST OFFICER: Affirmative.

1414:52.0

BOSTON CENTER: Maintain one nine zero, report reaching . . .

FIRST OFFICER: Roger.

1415:35.5

BOSTON CENTER: Clipper 160 is cleared direct to Boston.

1415:37.5

(SOUND OF ALTITUDE ALERT.)

FIRST OFFICER: Clipper 160 is cleared direct Boston.

BOSTON CENTER: Clipper 160 is cleared direct to Boston.

FIRST OFFICER: Cleared direct Boston, Clipper 160. Can you give me the landing runway please?

BOSTON CENTER: Clipper 160 squawk code one five zero zero.

1416:19.0

FIRST OFFICER: Squawking one five zero zero, level one nine zero.

1416:26.0

CAPTAIN (TO SEC-OND OFFICER): How does it look in the back, Dave?

1416:31.0

SECOND OFFICER: It's full [of smoke].

1416:56.0

CAPTAIN (TO SEC-OND OFFICER): Smoke detector showin' much?

SECOND OFFICER: No, ah, it's showin' the same as it was. We're somehow gettin' it [smoke] up through the floor from down below and it's goin' in the back, I think.

1417:24.0

BOSTON CENTER: Clipper 160, I don't know whether you received it. You're cleared direct to Boston.

FIRST OFFICER: Understand direct Boston. Do you read me?

BOSTON CENTER: Read you five-by now.

FIRST OFFICER: Thank you. And, ah, how far am I from Boston right now?

1418:04.0

BOSTON CENTER: Ah—a hundred miles, ah, out of Boston.

FIRST OFFICER: Okay, thank you.

CAPTAIN: Okay, I think we'll take it on in.

SECOND OFFICER: Just ease it on—it should be okay.

CAPTAIN: Right.

1418:40.5

BOSTON CENTER: 160, ah, what is your, ah, altitude now please and if I can be of assistance in any manner let me know.

1418:47.0

FIRST OFFICER:	Ah, we're at one nine zero and it's fine for us.
BOSTON CENTER:	Real fine day, okay, thank you.
FIRST OFFICER:	160, roger, stand by.

1419:01.0

CAPTAIN (TO BOSTON CENTER):	We'd like to get down as soon as possible so we can burn off some fuel. Boston from Clipper 160 . . .
BOSTON CENTER:	160 go ahead.
CAPTAIN:	Yes, sir, we'd like to get down as soon as possible so we can burn off some fuel rather than dump.
BOSTON CENTER:	Coordinatin' with the, ah, the, lower sector now. Clipper 160, descend and maintain one zero thousand.

1419:45.0

SECOND OFFICER (TO CAPTAIN):	I can't find a thing wrong back there.
CAPTAIN:	What's that?
SECOND OFFICER:	I can't find anything wrong.
CAPTAIN:	Okay, ah, maybe it's in a package.
SECOND OFFICER:	Could be.

1419:59.5

CAPTAIN:	Ah, you didn't get in to open the door into the back section, did you? Ah, they're supposed to be flame resistant or fire resistant anyhow, isn't it?
SECOND OFFICER:	Well I—I looked back there—the smoke—there's more smoke back there but there's none up here now. It must—it's in the Lower Forty-one someplace.
CAPTAIN:	I think so.

1420:32.0

BOSTON CENTER:	160, the Boston altimeter two nine seven five.
FIRST OFFICER:	Two nine seven five.
CAPTAIN:	Are we on vectors? It's direct Boston, wasn't it?
FIRST OFFICER:	Right.
SECOND OFFICER:	Want to make a normal landing out of it, Johnny?
CAPTAIN:	What's that?

SECOND OFFICER: Normal landing?

CAPTAIN: I think so, yeah.

SECOND OFFICER: Okay.

1421:11.5
BOSTON CENTER: 160, you anticipating flying, ah, locally to burn off fuel?

CAPTAIN: Ah, negative, we, negative we're coming right in.

BOSTON CENTER: Yes, sir.

CAPTAIN: Ah, we would like as low as possible to burn it off, as we're coming down and in.

1421:30.5
BOSTON CENTER: The Clipper 160, yuh got a rough, ah, ETA [Estimated Time of Arrival] Boston for me?

1421:35.0
CAPTAIN: Yes, it'll be, ah, ETA Boston about three five.

1421:45.5
BOSTON CENTER: 160, descend and maintain six thousand.

1421:46.5
FIRST OFFICER: Down to six thousand, Clipper 160.

1421:56.0
SECOND OFFICER (TO CAPTAIN): Maybe we should advise the fire department that we suspect electrical . . .

1421:58.5
BOSTON CENTER: 160, the, ah, Boston, ah, weather four thousand, ah, scattered, visibility fifteen plus, Runway 27 Left is available, the winds two eight zero, ah, stand by the winds, ah, two eight zero variable three one zero fifteen gusts two five, altimeter two nine seven, ah, five . . .

1422:21.0
CAPTAIN (TO FIRST OFFICER): How long is [Runway] 31 and how long is [Runway] 27?

FIRST OFFICER: 27 is seven thousand and 33 is ten thousand.

CAPTAIN: How much . . . you is, ah, 27?

FIRST OFFICER: Two seven—seven thousand, seven zero.

CAPTAIN: We'll take 31—33, Runway 33.

1422:40.0

BOSTON CENTER: Clipper 160, if you lose communications with me your backup frequency'll be one two eight point two.

FIRST OFFICER: Okay, one twenty-eight two if we lose contact with you—

BOSTON CENTER: Yes [sir].

FIRST OFFICER: And we'll be taking Runway 33, please.

BOSTON CENTER: I'll advise Boston Approach—and you want equipment standing by?

1423:03.0

FIRST OFFICER: Roger on the equipment. . . .

1423:13.0

SECOND OFFICER (TO CAPTAIN): Shall I advise the tower that we got a—that we suspect it's electrical in the forward end of the airplane?

CAPTAIN: What's Pan Ops [radio frequency]?

SECOND OFFICER: One twenty-nine eight. One twenty-nine seven, I think.

1423:30.5

FIRST OFFICER: Comin' up on six thousand [feet altitude].

1423:40.5

SECOND OFFICER (TO PAN AM OPERATIONS): Ah, Pan Op, Clipper 160.

PAN AM OPERA-TIONS: Clipper 160, go ahead, sir.

1423:48.0

SECOND OFFICER: Okay, we suspect this problem is electrical and it's in the forward end of the airplane. It's either in Lower Forty-one or the forward cargo hold, it seems like. There's quite a bit of smoke in the cockp—in the, ah—cabin.

1423:57.5

FIRST OFFICER: Boston Center, Clipper 160, can you get us down about two thousand feet, we're right in the clouds.

SECOND OFFICER: —but, ah, there doesn't, there isn't too much in the cockpit right now.

PAN AM OPERA- TIONS:	Ah, roger, roger, I have your equipment standing by, and what's your ETA, sir?
SECOND OFFICER:	About thirty-five and have 'em open the Lower Forty-one when we get there and, ah—stairs up the front door, it doesn't seem to be that much of a problem.
FIRST OFFICER:	Boston Center, Clipper 160 . . .
BOSTON CENTER:	160, go ahead.
FIRST OFFICER:	Can you get me down about two thousand feet?
BOSTON CENTER:	Stand by.
PAN AM OPERA- TIONS:	Roger, roger, stairs to the front door and open Lower Forty-one.

1424:20.0

SECOND OFFICER:	Thank you.
FIRST OFFICER:	Clipper 160 is requesting four thousand [feet altitude].
BOSTON CENTER:	160, understand four. We're trying to clear it now, and, ah, descend and maintain four thousand.

1424:42.0

FIRST OFFICER:	Cleared to four thousand, Clipper 160.
BOSTON CENTER:	Yuh out of five now?
CAPTAIN (TO FIRST OFFICER):	Keep an eye out for aircraft. There's a field down here (ALTITUDE ALERT SOUND.)
SECOND OFFICER:	Ready for the approach check . . . ?
CAPTAIN:	Yes, go ahead.
SECOND OFFICER:	Pressure altimeters.
CAPTAIN:	Twenty-nine seven five is okay.
FIRST OFFICER:	Set right.
SECOND OFFICER:	Set both times in the back.
CAPTAIN:	Landing bugs, we weigh two seventy-eight.
FIRST OFFICER:	Say again that landing gross weight.
SECOND OFFICER:	Okay, it was two seventy-eight but we're not burning it up very fast. Call it two seven five for landing.
CAPTAIN (TO FIRST OFFICER):	Ah, throw the [landing] gear out please.
FIRST OFFICER:	Gear coming dow—
CAPTAIN:	Hold it, hold it, I'm sorry, wait till I slow it down, we'll tear the doors off.

SECOND OFFICER:	Boy, this . . . won't slow down.

1427:10.5

FIRST OFFICER:	160's level at two thousand [feet].
BOSTON CENTER:	160, roger.
CAPTAIN:	Ah, yes, stand by one, put the gear down now please.

1427:30.0   (ALTITUDE ALERT.)

BOSTON CENTER:	160 has traffic at, ah, twelve o'clock four miles opposite direction, slow, altitude unknown.
FIRST OFFICER:	Okay, Clipper 160, ah, negative contact.
CAPTAIN:	What position was he in?
FIRST OFFICER:	I think he said twelve o'clock.
SECOND OFFICER:	Yeah, he did.

1427:59.0

CAPTAIN (TO SECOND OFFICER):	I don't smell that smoke as much now; there doesn't seem to be as much, does it?
SECOND OFFICER:	Ah—ah, it doesn't seem to be as much.
CAPTAIN:	Huh?
SECOND OFFICER:	It doesn't seem to be as much.

1428:25.0

SECOND OFFICER:	Okay, the engineer's check is complete, the approach check is complete, the landing is next.
CAPTAIN:	Okay, stand by.
FIRST OFFICER:	For the ILS [Instrument Landing System] you might wanna turn that three-thirty into your course selector.

1429:30.0

SECOND OFFICER:	Ah, it's [the smoke's] definitely comin' out of Lower Forty-one.
FIRST OFFICER:	Still coming out, huh?
SECOND OFFICER:	Yeah.
CAPTAIN:	Is it?
SECOND OFFICER:	It is.
CAPTAIN:	Okay.

1430:17.5

SECOND OFFICER:	That's worse. I don't see . . .
CAPTAIN:	It's getting worse.

1430:20.5

SECOND OFFICER: Ah, I turned the, ah, equipment cooler off and that—that made it worse.

CAPTAIN: Okay, then if that'll blow it out if you take the— keep it moving, won't it?

SECOND OFFICER: Yeah, I just pulled the breaker out again. I tried the CB to see if that'd do it, but the— Okay. It's, ah—

1430:36.5

CAPTAIN: All of a sudden it's getting worse in here.

SECOND OFFICER: Yeah. It's somewhere down in Lower Forty-one. Tell ya what, turn the radar off, the Doppler's off—anything yuh don't need, let's shut 'em down. That's off. Okay, it's VFR could I turn the, ah, ra—, radio altimeter [off]?

1431:18.0

FIRST OFFICER: Boston Approach Control, Clipper 160.

1431:20.5

BOSTON APPROACH CONTROL: 160, Bost—Approach Control, radar contact, thirty-five miles northeast of Boston, proceed direct Boston, maintain two thousand, and are you declaring an emergency?

1431:29.5

FIRST OFFICER: Negative on the emergency and, ah, may we have Runway 33 Left?

1431:33.0

BOSTON APPROACH CONTROL: That is correct, you can plan 33 Left, understand negative emergency, maintain two thousand and, ah, expect a visual approach to Runway 33 Left. The Boston altimeter is two niner seven three, the wind is two niner zero at one eight, the Boston weather four thousand scattered, visibility more than one five.

1431:50.5

FIRST OFFICER: Roger, roger Boston, Clipper 160.

1433:42.0

SECOND OFFICER: Doesn't seem to be gettin' any worse.

1433:44.5

CAPTAIN: No, but I don't think it's getting any better, is it?

1433:46.5
SECOND OFFICER: No, it's not getting any better.

1433:49.5
CAPTAIN: Beg pardon?

1433:51.0
SECOND OFFICER: It's not getting any better.

1433:51.0
CAPTAIN: No.

1433:52.0
FIRST OFFICER: It's getting worse right now. You can see it blowin' around here.

1433:54.0
SECOND OFFICER: Yeah.
CAPTAIN: Yeah.

1433:58.5
FIRST OFFICER: Gear up?

1434:01.0
CAPTAIN: Naw, I want to burn fuel.

1434:15.0
SECOND OFFICER: Okay, landing gear.

1434:18.0
FIRST OFFICER: Down three green.

1434:20.0
BOSTON APPROACH CONTROL: Clipper 160, what do you show for a compass heading right now?

1434:23.0
FIRST OFFICER: Compass heading at this time is two zero five.

1434:26.0
BOSTON APPROACH CONTROL: Okay, fine, and will you accept a vector for a visual approach to a five mile final, ah, will that be sat—compatible with you?

1434:35.5
FIRST OFFICER: What was that, Approach?

1436:36.5

BOSTON
APPROACH CON-
TROL:

Will you accept a vector for a visual approach to a five mile final for Runway 33 Left, or do you want to be extended out further?

1434:43.0

CAPTAIN:

Ah, negative, we want to get in as soon as possible.

1434:46.5

BOSTON
APPROACH CON-
TROL:

Okay, proceed to the Boston VOR, advise when you have the airport in sight. Clipper 160, you're number one for Runway 33 Left.

1434:53.5

FIRST OFFICER:

Roger, Clipper 160.

1434:55.5

BOSTON
APPROACH CON-
TROL:

Are you able to maintain two thou—

1434:57.5

FIRST OFFICER:

That's affirmative. . . .

1434:58.5

BOSTON
APPROACH CON-
TROL:

Okay, fine. There will be traffic at ten o'clock, one zero miles westbound . . . an Air Canada Viscount descending to three [thousand feet].

1435:05.5

FIRST OFFICER:

Roger. [Last radio transmission received from Pan Am Flight 160.]

1435:46.0

BOSTON
APPROACH CON-
TROL:

Clipper 160, advise anytime you have the airport in sight.

1440:06.0   (SOUND OF IMPACT.)

As Pan Am 160 approached Boston's Logan Airport, the Captain opened the left cockpit window. Smoke billowed out. Approaching Runway 27 at a faster-than-normal speed, the aircraft assumed a final nose-high, then an abrupt nose-down, attitude. The left wing and the nose simultaneously hit the ground. At impact, Pan Am 160 was nearly vertical. All three crew members suffered fatal injuries. The aircraft was destroyed.

1440:23.0

BOSTON
  APPROACH CON-
  TROL:

All aircraft on the frequency, the airport is closed.

9. Southern Airways Flight 932 (SOU 932)

Southern Airways Flight 932, a DC-9 charter, was transporting the Marshall University football team and boosters, seventy-four passengers in all, from Kinston, North Carolina, to Huntington, West Virginia, on 14 November 1970. As it attempted a nonprecision instrument landing approach to Runway 11 of the Tri-State Airport, Huntington, SOU 932 ran into trouble.

1916:59.9

CAPTAIN:	Charleston Tower, this is Southern 932.
CHARLESTON TOWER:	Southern 932, Charleston Tower.
CAPTAIN:	We're going over to Huntington. We passed just south of Charleston. What kind of weather you got down there now?
CHARLESTON TOWER:	Charleston weather estimated ceiling six thousand broken, visibility four, ground fog and smoke.
CAPTAIN:	What's your spread?
CHARLESTON TOWER:	Temperature five zero, dew point four nine.
CAPTAIN:	Thank you. Look like it's going to hold up awhile?
CHARLESTON TOWER:	Sure thing.

1919:00.2

FIRST OFFICER:	Southern 932 out of eleven thousand five hundred.
CAPTAIN:	Approach plate's two years old.
FIRST OFFICER:	Yeah. . . . On these charter kits they don't keep those things up like they're supposed to. (SOUND OF LAUGHTER.)

CAPTAIN (CONTACTS INDIANAPOLIS CENTER, WHICH HAS PICKED UP RADAR CONTROL OF SOUTHERN 932):	Center, Southern 932.

1921:57.3

INDIANAPOLIS CENTER:	Southern 932, descend and maintain five thousand, say again.

1922:02.7

FIRST OFFICER:	Okay, Southern 932, we're out of eight now. We're going to five, and approximately how far do you show us from the Huntington Airport?

1922:09.7

INDIANAPOLIS CENTER:	932, approximately twenty miles southeast of Huntington Airport.
FIRST OFFICER:	Roger.
INDIANAPOLIS CENTER:	Southern 932, squawk zero four zero zero, contact Huntington Approach Control one two zero point niner, radar service terminated.
SECOND OFFICER:	One two zero point nine, good day, sir.
CAPTAIN:	Here we go.
FIRST OFFICER:	Huntington Approach, Southern 932, we're descending to five thousand.
HUNTINGTON APPROACH CONTROL:	Southern 932, Huntington Approach Control, you're cleared for an approach, correction, you're cleared for a localizer [Runway] 11 approach, the surface wind's favoring Runway 29, wind three five zero degrees at six, altimeter two nine six seven, report leaving five thousand. I'll give you the weather shortly.
FIRST OFFICER:	Okay, we got the altimeter and we'll check with you leaving five thousand, we plan on approach to [Runway] 11.
HUNTINGTON APPROACH CONTROL:	Roger. (SOUND OF INSTRUMENT LANDING SYSTEM LOCALIZER IDENTIFICATION.) Southern 932, the Huntington weather three hundred scattered, measured ceiling five hundred, variable broken, one thousand one hundred overcast, visibility five, light rain, fog, smoke. Ceiling ragged, variable four to six hundred.

CAPTAIN (TO FIRST OFFICER):	Phew!
FIRST OFFICER:	Very well, thank you, sir.
CAPTAIN:	Very well!
FIRST OFFICER:	Four hundred and twelve.
CAPTAIN:	Yeah, and a mile visibility.
FIRST OFFICER:	He said the visibility was . . . ? I'll ask him again. What's your visibility again?
HUNTINGTON APPROACH CONTROL:	Visibility five [miles], light rain, fog, smoke.
FIRST OFFICER:	Right.
CAPTAIN:	Right on the . . . right on the minimums. See if you can get that thing tuned in a little bit better, sort of wavering.
FIRST OFFICER:	All right. Southern 932 is out of five.

1924:15.7

HUNTINGTON APPROACH CONTROL:	Out of five [thousand feet], report outer marker outbound.
FIRST OFFICER:	Localizer is one zero nine nine . . . one fourteen inbound.
CAPTAIN:	Wonder how many miles it is to Kanawha?
FIRST OFFICER:	Stand by. Charleston's not but about fifty miles. Ought to be getting pretty damn close 'cause he gave us twenty miles right back there. That's been four or five minutes.
SECOND OFFICER (TO CAPTAIN):	Frank, you want full fuel load out of here?
CAPTAIN:	Might as well.
FIRST OFFICER:	Minimum is nineteen. . . . Wonder how much they'll charge us?
SECOND OFFICER:	Well, we got contract price, whatever that is, whatever we pay for it.
FIRST OFFICER:	We got a mile or two to go, Frank, is all.
SECOND OFFICER:	Hope we don't have this [weather] all the way in. It's rough.

1927:58.9

FIRST OFFICER:	There she is. [To Huntington Approach Control]: Southern 932, we're over the marker now, proceeding outbound.

HUNTINGTON APPROACH CON-TROL:	Southern 932, roger, report the marker inbound.
CAPTAIN:	Slats and five [degrees of flaps].

1928:11.0

FIRST OFFICER:	Very well.

1928:35.6

CAPTAIN:	Slats and five. [From the] lights on the ground [it looks like] fog.
FIRST OFFICER:	Makes it sorry, doesn't it?

1930:03.0

FIRST OFFICER:	[I believe] half those lights should be off to our left. Kinda hard to say, though.

1930:43.6

CAPTAIN:	We're in a rain shower, all right.
FIRST OFFICER:	Yeah, I know it.

1930:49.6

CAPTAIN:	We sure are. The temp [is dropping].
FIRST OFFICER:	Yeah, ah, that rain is [mixed] in with fog. (SOUND OF WINDSHIELD WIPERS COMMENCES; SOUND OF LANDING GEAR IN TRANSIT COMMENCES.) Okay, you got the no smoking, ignition, radar standby, auto shutoff armed, waiting on the gear—got the spoilers?
CAPTAIN:	Armed. (SOUND OF CLICK SIMILAR TO THAT OF ARMING SPOILERS.)
FIRST OFFICER:	Checked [spoilers are] out.
CAPTAIN:	You getting a glide slope capture and you ain't got a glide slope.
FIRST OFFICER:	I might capture on the, ah, on ILS, ah, Frank, regardless of glide slope. I don't have no capture, though.

1931:49.8

CAPTAIN:	Okay, give me, ah, twenty-five [degrees flaps].
FIRST OFFICER:	Yeah, it's good, it's got the capture.
CAPTAIN:	I got it cut off there now.
FIRST OFFICER:	Got twenty-five flaps, all is squared.
CAPTAIN:	We ought to be over the outer marker at twenty . . . two hundred feet.
FIRST OFFICER:	Yeah.

CAPTAIN (TO FIRST OFFICER):	You going to call out minimums?
FIRST OFFICER:	Yeah, I sure will. I'll sing 'em out to you. As you get on down it, ah, this rough air ought to give us a little break.
CAPTAIN:	Well, if it's like he said, it's not blowing any harder than he says it is, why—
FIRST OFFICER:	Down draft.
CAPTAIN:	It took us down to the marker level. Must be a little rain shower.

1933:19.9

FIRST OFFICER:	Back in the soup.
CAPTAIN:	Jerry, I'm going to be flying about one-thirty.
FIRST OFFICER:	I'm going to check the time for you. It'll be about two minutes from the, ah, outer marker. (SOUND OF OUTER MARKER BEGINS; SOUND OF OUTER MARKER CEASES ABRUPTLY.) Southern 932, the marker inbound.
HUNTINGTON APPROACH CONTROL:	Southern 932 is cleared to land. You can advise on the lights. The wind is now three four zero degrees seven.

1933:59.1

FIRST OFFICER:	Okay, the lights be good about step three, I guess.
HUNTINGTON APPROACH CONTROL:	Roger, that's where they are, with the rabbit. Advise when you want them cut.
FIRST OFFICER:	Very good.
CAPTAIN:	This autopilot ain't responding just right—sluggish.
FIRST OFFICER:	Yeah.
CAPTAIN:	Might catch up.
FIRST OFFICER:	Okay, I got the time for you. A thousand feet above the ground, rate and speed good. Speed a little fast, looks good, got bug and twelve.

1934:55.4

CAPTAIN:	See something?
SECOND OFFICER:	No, not yet. It's beginning to lighten up a little bit on the ground here at, ah, ah, seven hundred feet. Bug and five. We're two hundred above.

1935:10.6

SECOND OFFICER:	Bet it'll be a missed approach.

1935:18.2
FIRST OFFICER: Four hundred [feet].

1935:19.3
CAPTAIN: That the approach?
FIRST OFFICER: Yeah. Hundred and twenty-six [feet].

1935:25.7
FIRST OFFICER: *Hundred* [feet].

1935:32.5   (SOUND OF IMPACT.)

Southern 932 impacted with treetops on a hill approximately one mile west of the runway's threshold. The elevation of the treetops at the initial impact site was approximately 922 feet. All seventy-five occupants, including seventy-one passengers and four crew members, were fatally injured. The aircraft was destroyed.

10. Northwest Airlines Flight 6231 (NWA 6231)

ON 1 DECEMBER 1974, Northwest Airlines Flight 6231, a Boeing 727-251, was a ferry flight from JFK International Airport to Buffalo, New York. With three crew members and no passengers aboard, Flight 6231 departed JFK about 1914 hours on a standard instrument departure, then climbed to 14,000 feet. At 1920:21, New York Air Route Traffic Control Center assumed radar control of the flight. At 1921:07, Flight 6231 was cleared to climb to 31,000 feet. Flight 6231 proceeded without reported difficulty until 1924:42, when a crew member transmitted, "Mayday, Mayday..." New York Air Route Traffic Control Center responded, "... Go ahead." And the crew member said, "Roger, we're out of control, descending through twenty thousand feet." Another company airplane, Northwest Flight 233, then took up the search and the vigil.

1912:05

NWA 6231:   Northwest 6231 is ready to sequence.

LOCAL CONTROL: Roger.

1912:25

LOCAL CONTROL: Northwest 6231, position and hold 4 Left.

NWA 6231:   Position and hold Northwest 6231.

1913:25

LOCAL CONTROL: Northwest 6231, ah, cleared for takeoff.

NWA 6231:   Here we go.

1914:25

LOCAL CONTROL: Northwest 6231, contact Departure Control.

1914:40

NWA 6231:   Northwest 6231, twelve hundred feet.

1914:45
JFK DEPARTURE: Northwest 6231, Kennedy, climb and maintain one zero thousand.

1915:00
NWA 6231: Northwest 6231 is going to ten [thousand feet].

1915:06
JFK DEPARTURE: Northwest 6231, roger. Northwest 6231 turn left zero four zero.

1915:40
NWA 6231: Zero four zero for 6231.

1917:10
JFK DEPARTURE: Northwest 6231, continue climb to one four thousand report [garbled] leaving eleven.

1917:25
NWA 6231: [Garbled.] Okay, and fourteen thousand, Northwest 6231.

1918:50
JFK DEPARTURE: Northwest 6231, turn left to three six zero and intercept the Huguenot [navigational beacon] one two eight radial.

1918:55
NWA 6231: North to intercept the one two eight and we're out of eleven, Northwest 6231.

1919:05
NEW YORK (AIR ROUTE TRAFFIC CONTROL) CENTER: Radar.

1920:05
JFK DEPARTURE: Northwest 6231, New York Center on one three two, correction, one three three point two.

1920:10
NWA 6231: Three three two, so long.

1920:35
NEW YORK CENTER: Northwest 6231, radar contact.

NWA 6231: Okay.

1921:05

NEW YORK CENTER: Northwest 6231, climb mountain flight level three one zero.

NWA 6231: Three one zero, Northwest 6231.

1924:40

NWA 6231: Mayday! Mayday! Northwest 6231, over.

NEW YORK CENTER: 6231 go ahead.

1924:50

NWA 6231: Roger, out of control . . . descending through twenty thousand feet.

NEW YORK CENTER: Northwest 6231, descend maintain flight level two zero zero.

1925:00

NWA 6231: Roger, we're below eighteen thousand feet at this time. [Pause] Okay. . . .

1925:20

NEW YORK CENTER: Northwest 6231, what is your problem, sir?

1925:23

NWA 6231: We're descending through twelve [thousand feet]. We're in a stall.

1925:25

NEW YORK CENTER: Northwest 6231, roger.

1925:45

NEW YORK CENTER: Northwest 6231, New York . . .

1925:50

NEW YORK CENTER: (TO ANOTHER NORTHWEST FLIGHT IN THE AREA): Northwest 233, you have company traffic at three o'clock eight miles southbound. He declared an emergency. I'm not working him right now.

NWA 233: We're right in the weather. Would you like us to take a heading?

NEW YORK CENTER: That's affirmative, sir. If you would turn right to a heading of about three-fifty.

NWA 233: Three five zero heading, Northwest 233.

NEW YORK CENTER: Northwest 233, roger. Would you like to try to pick up this company traffic, sir?

NWA 233: Yes, sir, I'll try.

NEW YORK CENTER: Okay, continue your turn to a three-sixty heading.

NWA 233: Okay, a three-sixty for, ah, three six [unintelligible] for Northwest 233.

NEW YORK CENTER: Affirmative three-sixty heading.

1926:20

NWA 233: Okay.

1926:35

NEW YORK CENTER: Northwest 233, I've lost your company's traffic.

NWA 233: Roger, 6231 from Northwest 233, do you read?

1926:45

NEW YORK CENTER: Northwest 6231, New York Center on guard. If you hear, squawk seven seven zero zero.

1926:55

NWA 233: Northwest 6231 from Northwest 233, do you read?

1927:00

NEW YORK CENTER: Northwest 233, your company traffic's last known position's about one o'clock and four miles, sir.

1927:10

NWA 233: Roger. [Pause.] We're in the weather. Northwest 6231 from Northwest 233, do you read, sir?

1927:25

NEW YORK CENTER: Northwest 233, I've lost your company [Flight 6231] on the frequency, ah, correction, on the radar. If you'd like to stay in the area you can make a three-sixty there in your present position.

NWA 233: Say again your last remarks.

NEW YORK CENTER: Northwest 233, I've lost your company on the radar, sir, if you like you can make a three-sixty in your present area.

1927:50
NWA 233:   Okay, just a second.

1927:55
NEW YORK CENTER: Northwest 6231, New York. Northwest 233, ah, your company has been lost in radar, sir, and I've lost radio with him. He was about five miles west of Bear Mountain intersection when I lost him in the radar.

1928:35
NWA 233:   Okay.

1929:00
NEW YORK CENTER: Northwest 233, New York Center on guard. If you hear, squawk seven seven zero zero.

1929:25
NWA 233:   Center, Northwest 233 . . .

NEW YORK CENTER: Northwest 233, go ahead.

NWA 233:   Would you want us to go present position direct Huguenot on course and he's like higher altitude, please.

NEW YORK CENTER: Northwest 233, roger. Turn left heading two seven zero. I'll have higher for you in a moment, sir.

NWA 233:   Okay.

NEW YORK CENTER: Northwest 233, intercept the Huguenot three twelve. Resume navigation.

NWA 233:   Say again for 233.

NEW YORK CENTER: Northwest 233, fly heading of two seven zero intercept Huguenot three one two radial.

NWA 233:   Okay, the three one two radial.

NEW YORK CENTER: Northwest 233, roger. Thank you for your help. I'll have higher for you in a moment.

1930:05
NWA 233:   Okay, [Pause.] Ah, we're in the weather in our present position and as we were a few miles back and I can just barely see anything outside.

NEW YORK CENTER: Northwest 233, roger.

NWA 233:   Occasionally we can see the ground but we sure couldn't see anything when we were back a little ways.

1930:25

NEW YORK CENTER:	Northwest 233, roger. Climb and maintain one seven thousand.
NWA 233:	Cleared to seventeen and we're out of ten, Northwest 233.

1930:50

NEW YORK CENTER:	Northwest 233, climb and maintain flight level three five zero.
NWA 233:	Cleared to three five zero, Northwest 233.

1931:30

NEW YORK CENTER:	Northwest 233, would you estimate the flight conditions, sir?
NWA 233:	We just broke out of a, ah, ah, broken overcast layer at about, ah, eleven point five and I would say that we were between layers at ten and it was broken by the time . . .

1931:45

NEW YORK CENTER:	Roger, sir.

1932:45

NEW YORK CENTER:	Northwest 233, turn right heading three two zero, intercept Huguenot three twelve.
NWA 233:	Okay, three twenty to intercept the Huguenot three twelve, Northwest 233.

1933:25

NEW YORK CENTER:	Northwest 6231, Northwest 6231, New York Center, do you read?

1935:55

NEW YORK CENTER:	Northwest 233, contact New York now on one thirty-two one.
NWA 233:	Okay, thirty-two point one.

At 1925:57, the aircraft, NWA 6231, had crashed in a forest in Harriman State Park, about 3.2 miles west of Thiells, New York. No one witnessed the crash because the accident had occurred at night. All three crew members were critically injured. The aircraft was destroyed.

11. *Republic Airlines Flight 303 (RC 303)*

On 2 April 1983, Republic Flight 303, a DC-9-80, on a scheduled flight from Minneapolis to Los Angeles, while flying at 35,000 feet approximately twenty miles north of Bryce, Utah, experienced flameout of both engines. There were 139 passengers and a crew of 7 aboard.

2303:10 GMT
RC 303:   Center, Republic 303, level three five zero, clear.

2303:13
SALT LAKE   Republic 303, Salt Lake Center, roger.
  CENTER:

2310:40
SALT LAKE   Republic 303, left heading two three zero.
  CENTER:

2310:44
RC 303:   Two three zero, Republic 303.

2313:09
RC 303:   Center, Republic—three zero three.

2313:09
SALT LAKE   Republic 303, go ahead.
  CENTER:

2313:11
RC 303:   Yeah, we just had an emergency. We had a double engine flameout.

2313:16
SALT LAKE
  CENTER:

Ya got a *double* engine out?

2313:20
RC 303:

That's correct. Yes, sir, that's correct.

2313:25
SALT LAKE
  CENTER:

Okay, are you going to be able to hold your altitude at all?

2313:27
RC 303:

Negative; that's all we have is two [engines].

2313:35
SALT LAKE
  CENTER:

If you make any turns, make them to the left, 303.

2313:39
RC 303:

Roger, I understand a turn to the left?

2313:41
SALT LAKE
  CENTER:

Yeah, if you need to go down, yeah, ah, you descending now?

2313:44
RC 303:

That's affirm——

2314:43
SALT LAKE
  CENTER:

Republic 303, Salt Lake, how do you, ah, what's your altitude now?

2314:53
RC 303:

Where would you like Republic 303 to head?

2314:55
SALT LAKE
  CENTER:

Okay, ah—well, we got Bryce Canyon Airport there. I don't know if it, ah, be long enough runway for you or not. Let me check right quick.

2315:48
SALT LAKE
  CENTER:

Ah, Page, Arizona, is there at your, ah, just due south of you there at sixty-four. It probably will be better for you. . . .

2315:56
RC 303:

Okay, we will take that, give us a heading for that. Give us a heading for that.

2316:05
SALT LAKE
CENTER:

Roger, ah, heading one eight five.

2316:09
RC 303:

Roger. Ah, we are try—trying to get one engine started.

2316:28
SALT LAKE
CENTER:

Okay, you are still trying to get one, ah, started, is that correct?

2316:31
RC 303:

Right.

2316:32
SALT LAKE
CENTER:

Roger . . .

2316:34
RC 303:

How far is this airport from us?

2316:43
SALT LAKE
CENTER:

Yeah, Page is, ah, about, no wind heading now of, ah, sixty miles.

2316:48
RC 303:

Okay.

2316:51
SALT LAKE
CENTER:

And, ah, Bryce Canyon is off to the west and I got a lot of wind. I think you will be better for Page, Arizona.

2316:57
RC 303:

Okay, we'll try that.

2317:07
SALT LAKE
CENTER:

And 303, can you give me an altitude?

2317:52
SALT LAKE
CENTER:

And Republic 303, that Page, ah, ah, Arizona is fifty-five hundred feet.

2317:58
RC 303:

Okay, well. We'll have to try it.

2318:02
SALT LAKE
  CENTER:
And further right heading one nine zero.

2318:06
RC 303:
One nine zero.

2318:07
SALT LAKE
  CENTER:
Roger, and what is your present altitude?

2318:10
RC 303:
We're at twenty-four hundred . . . thousand. . . .

2318:12
SALT LAKE
  CENTER:
Twenty-four *thousand*. Roger.

2318:13
RC 303:
Twenty-four thousand.

2318:57
SALT LAKE
  CENTER:
And Republic 303, ah—Bryce Canyon Airport is, ah, no wind heading two five two, forty miles and, ah, you could land on Runway 21 with a seven-thousand-foot runway.

2319:10
RC 303:
Say again how far it is.

2319:13
SALT LAKE
  CENTER:
Yeah, it's, ah, thirty-seven miles due west.

2319:16
RC 303:
And how far is the one straight ahead?

2319:23
SALT LAKE
  CENTER:
Forty-two [miles]. And a little bit more—if I turn you into the wind there, ah, I don't know what the surface wind, at high altitude, winds are about a hundred knots, ah, hundred and twenty knots at thirty-five, so I think you'd be better for Page.

2319:42
RC 303:
Okay, we'll stick with Page.

2319:43
SALT LAKE
  CENTER:

Roger and further right one niner five.

2319:46
RC 303:

All right one ninety-five.

2320:22
SALT LAKE
  CENTER:

And Republic 303, your minimum safe altitude between your position and Page is, ah, one zero thousand. Republic 303, did you copy?

2320.39
RC 303:

That's affirmative, we copied.

2320:40
SALT LAKE
  CENTER:

Roger. Republic 303, ah, Page, ah, Airport is twelve o'clock and three eight miles.

2321:10
RC 303:

Say again.

2321:12
SALT LAKE
  CENTER:

Twelve o'clock and three eight miles.

2321:14
RC 303:

Okay, which side of the, ah, lake is it?

2321:23
SALT LAKE
  CENTER:

Yeah, it's on the south side of the lake.

2321:25
RC 303:

Okay, thank you.

2322:12
SALT LAKE
  CENTER:

And Republic 303, ah, the airport is, ah, on the north and, ah, east side of the lake.

2322:26
RC 303:

Republic 303, Salt Lake . . . okay, on the north and east side?

2322:35
SALT LAKE
  CENTER:

That's affirm.

2323:19
SALT LAKE
  CENTER:

Republic 303, twelve o'clock and two eight miles.

2323:22
RC 303:

Roger.

2323:56
SALT LAKE
  CENTER:

And Republic 303, runway direction is three hundred and one two at, ah, Page. Republic 303, what's your present altitude?

2324:05.1
RC 303:

Okay, we're out of fourteen thousand four hundred [feet].

2324:07
SALT LAKE
  CENTER:

Roger. And 303, you still in the clouds?

2324:17.3
RC 303:

We're in the clear.

2324:20
SALT LAKE
  CENTER:

You're in the clear. And Republic 303 twelve o'clock and two zero miles.

2324:57.7
RC 303:

Okay, we're looking, we don't see an airport yet.

2325.02
SALT LAKE
  CENTER:

And altimeter two niner six seven and the airport is clear.

2325:08.6
RC 303:

Two niner two seven?

2325:10
SALT LAKE
  CENTER:

Two niner *six* seven on the altimeter. Okay, and the runway, ah, direction is three three and one five.

2325:22.3
RC 303:

Thank you.

2325:24
SALT LAKE
  CENTER:

Wind is zero four, ah, five degrees. Elevation of the, ah, Page Airport is forty-three ten.

2326:23.9

RC 303:

Okay, the engines are restarted now. We are leveling off here and, ah, we like to press on at least to the other airport, the longer one you were telling us about, ah, off to the right. Copy that Center?

2326:45

SALT LAKE
CENTER:

Republic 303, roger, understand you got, ah, engines started, ah, looks like you are maintaining your altitude. Can you maintain your present altitude now?

2326:53.7

RC 303:

Yeah, we can do that. Ah, we can climb a little bit. We don't want to go too much higher, however.

2326:58

SALT LAKE
CENTER:

Roger, just maintain your present altitude and, ah, we can either give you Bryce Canyon or take you over to Cedar City. That might be your best bet.

2327:12.2

RC 303:

I think Bryce Canyon would probably be the best choice here. We are going to see if we can talk to company or someone here. Do you want to give us a heading to Bryce Canyon here?

2327:26

SALT LAKE
CENTER:

Republic 303, ah, right heading two nine five.

2327:34.8

RC 303:

Two nine five, roger.

After consulting with their company representatives on the ground, Republic 303 decided to fly past Bryce Canyon and landed safely at Las Vegas International Airport. The probable cause of the engine failure was poor fuel management. In Las Vegas, all 146 passengers and crew exited the aircraft without injury.

12. *North Central Airlines Flight 458 (NCA 458)*

ON 27 DECEMBER 1968, North Central Airlines Flight 458, an Allison Prop-Jet Convair CV-580, a regularly scheduled passenger flight originating in Minneapolis and terminating at O'Hare International Airport, Chicago, with en route stops, was cleared to descend to 6,000 feet by the Chicago Air Traffic Control Center and was handed off to O'Hare Approach Control. The controller instructed the flight to turn left to a heading of 090 degrees for a radar vector to the Instrument Landing System for Runway 14 Right. The flight was then cleared to descend to 3,500 feet and reported leaving 6,000 feet. The controller instructed Flight 458 with its forty-five passengers and crew to slow to 180 knots.

0214:06

O'HARE ARRIVAL RADAR: North Central 458, turn right heading one-twenty, intercept the 14R [Romeo] ILS, fly it inbound, cleared for the approach, cne-sixty till Romeo, RVR [Runway Visual Range] four thousand, position from Romeo is fourteen miles.

FIRST OFFICER: Roger, North Central 458, that heading one two zero, take over on the approach, one-sixty to Romeo.

0214:26.5

O'HARE ARRIVAL RADAR: Roger.

FIRST OFFICER: Down to twenty-five hundred [feet]. Fourteen miles out. Comin' in on the localizer.

0215:30.0

O'HARE ARRIVAL RADAR: RVR 14 Right, North Central 458, two thousand six hundred [feet].

FIRST OFFICER:	Okay.
O'HARE ARRIVAL RADAR:	What do you need, twenty-four [hundred feet]?
CAPTAIN (TO FIRST OFFICER):	Yeah.
FIRST OFFICER (TO CAPTAIN):	Now, wait a minute now.
CAPTAIN (TO FIRST OFFICER):	Yeah.
FIRST OFFICER (TO CAPTAIN):	Ah, yes, sir.

0215:41.5

O'HARE ARRIVAL RADAR:	Okay.
FIRST OFFICER:	No, we can go to eighteen [hundred feet].
CAPTAIN:	Eighteen? Shows twenty-four in my book.
FIRST OFFICER:	I got eighteen in my book.
CAPTAIN:	Have you?
FIRST OFFICER:	Yes, sir. Right here. Full ILS.
CAPTAIN:	Okay.
FIRST OFFICER:	As long as they got all components working. Twenty-five hundred feet we are. . . . All components are working. We're good for eighteen hundred, Marv.
CAPTAIN:	How about the glide path?
FIRST OFFICER:	Gotta have center line and touchdown.
CAPTAIN:	Both of them? What date on that, Jerr?
FIRST OFFICER:	Huh?
CAPTAIN:	What date you got on your—
FIRST OFFICER:	—on the Approach Plate, December twenty, sixty-eight.
CAPTAIN:	[Won]der what mine is.
FIRST OFFICER:	We're about five [miles] out from Romeo.
CAPTAIN:	Yeah.

0217:26.5

O'HARE ARRIVAL RADAR:	North Central 458 is three and a half [miles] behind traffic that's four [miles] from the marker, and the tower is one eighteen one at Romeo, RVR is three thousand eight hundred.
FIRST OFFICER:	458, one eighteen one at the marker.

0217:37.6

O'HARE ARRIVAL RADAR:	Roger.
FIRST OFFICER:	Four [miles] for the lock-on. Down to twenty-two hundred.
CAPTAIN:	Fifteen degrees [flaps].
FIRST OFFICER:	Okay, you got it, two two hundred [feet].
O'HARE ARRIVAL RADAR:	We got RVR two thousand eight hundred now.
FIRST OFFICER:	We got twenty-eight hundred RVR. . . . (SOUND OF OUTER MARKER COMMENCES, SOFTLY, THEN GRADUALLY INCREASES.)
FIRST OFFICER:	. . . Coming up on the outer marker. (SOUND OF LANDING GEAR WARNING HORN.)
CAPTAIN:	Twenty-four [hundred feet]. Gear and landing check.
FIRST OFFICER:	They're both on now. Smoker's on. Temp trim is three caps. Three green. Brakes?
CAPTAIN:	Off.
FIRST OFFICER:	Yaw damper.
CAPTAIN:	Off.
FIRST OFFICER:	Landing check's complete.
CAPTAIN:	One twenty [knots]?
FIRST OFFICER:	Ah, one fifteen [knots].
CAPTAIN:	Twenty-eight [hundred feet]. (SOUND OF OUTER MARKER CEASES ABRUPTLY.)
FIRST OFFICER:	Twenty-eight [RVR] coming.

0219:28.8

O'HARE ARRIVAL RADAR:	North Central 458, number two, 14 Right, the RVR forty-five hundred.
FIRST OFFICER:	Okay. Pretty good.
CAPTAIN:	Yeah. One fifteen [knots], huh?
FIRST OFFICER:	One fifteen.
O'HARE LOCAL CONTROL (TO AN AMERICAN AIRLINE TAXIING FOR TAKEOFF):	American 254, are you here?

0219:41.1

NCA 458 FIRST OFFICER:	[We are] below the glide path. . . .
NCA 458 CAPTAIN:	. . . Yeah . . .

NCA 458 FIRST OFFICER:	. . . a little bit.
NCA 458 SECOND OFFICER:	Never captured the son of a buck.

0220:02.6

O'HARE LOCAL CONTROL:	North Central 458 cleared to land 14 Right.

0220:05.0

NCA 458 FIRST OFFICER:	She'll fly the glide path.
AA 254:	Chicago, American 254 approaching, ah, 14 Left. Ready for takeoff?
O'HARE LOCAL CONTROL:	American 254, okay, let me know when you're right up at the runway.
AA 254:	Wilco.
O'HARE LOCAL CONTROL (TO NORTHWEST FLIGHT 716):	Northwest 716, right to one eight zero, contact Departure.
NWA 716:	Oh, that's 716, roger, change over.
O'HARE LOCAL CONTROL:	American 254, taxi into position 14 Left.
AA 254:	Position and hold, American, ah, 254, we're just coming up to make the, ah, first right turn right now.
NCA 458 CAPTAIN:	About nine hundred [feet] on 'er, Jerry?
O'HARE LOCAL CONTROL (TO AA 254):	Okay, after departure it'll be a left turn to zero nine zero.
NCA 458 SECOND OFFICER:	Okay, nine hundred.
AA 254:	Understand zero nine zero after takeoft

0221:24.4

TRANS WORLD FLIGHT 28 ON FINAL APPROACH:	TWA 28 is Romeo inbound.
O'HARE LOCAL CONTROL:	TWA 28, O'Hare, number two, continue approach.
NCA 458 CAPTAIN:	Least they're running us in pretty tight.
TWA 28:	TWA 28 . . .

0221:30.9

NCA 458 FIRST OFFICER:	Ah, you're coming up on five hundred feet, a hundred and eighteen, sinking five, occasional ground contract.

NCA 458 SECOND OFFICER:	Pretty good.
NCA 458 FIRST OFFICER:	Four hundred feet, one eighteen, sinking five, approach lights twelve o'clock in sight. (BEGINNING TO RAIN; SOUND OF WINDSHIELD WIPER COMMENCES.)
NCA 458 CAPTAIN:	See the runway yet?
NCA 458 FIRST OFFICER:	No, not yet.

0221:51.7

NCA 458 FIRST OFFICER:	There, you're high.

0221:57.7

NCA 458 FIRST OFFICER:	On a hundred . . .
O'HARE LOCAL CONTROL (TO TAXIING EASTERN FLIGHT 229):	Eastern 229 up to the runway but hold short.

0222:03.0

NCA 458 CAPTAIN:	*Nine seventy-one, four thousand, flaps fifteen!*
EA 229:	Two twenty-nine.
AA 254:	American 254 is, ah, on the runway and about to hold in position.

0222:11.7

NCA 458 CAPTAIN:	*Gear up!*
O'HARE LOCAL CONTROL (TO AA 254):	Okay, I'll have a release for you just shortly.
AA 254:	Okay.

0222:17.2

NCA 458 CAPTAIN:	*You got nine seventy-one on 'er?*
NCA 458 FIRST OFFICER:	*You got it all, Dad! We're gonna hit!*

0222:23.8   (SOUND OF IMPACT.)

The NCA 458 hit the main door of a hangar located approximately sixteen hundred feet from the left edge of the runway and approximately one hundred feet southeast of the threshold. Twenty-seven of the forty-five passengers and crew on board died. The aircraft was destroyed.

13. Trans World Airlines Flight 5787 (TWA 5787)

On 26 July 1969, Flight 5787, a Boeing 707-331C Cargojet powered by four Pratt and Whitney JT-30 fanjet engines, departed JFK International Airport for training and proficiency checks for three TWA Captains. The first Captain to receive the proficiency check occupied the left seat, an Instructor-Pilot occupied the right seat, and a Flight Engineer occupied the flight engineer's position. The other two Captains observed while awaiting their turn at the controls. The flight went from JFK to Atlantic City Airport, Pomona, New Jersey. Atlantic City Approach Control vectored the aircraft to the outer marker for an approach to and a full-stop landing on Runway 13. TWA 5787 requested to taxi to the end of the runway, turn, and take off on Runway 13. Before takeoff, the Instructor-Pilot briefed the Captain to expect a simulated engine failure after V-1, or the decision speed of the aircraft, then to execute a three-engine climb-out. The Number Four engine was spooled down to idle thrust after V-1 on the takeoff roll. Emergency procedures were executed. The aircraft leveled off at 1,500 feet. The Number Four engine remained in idle thrust. The Instructor-Pilot then directed the Captain to execute a simulated three-engine approach and to expect a missed approach at the decision height, just before landing. As TWA 5787 neared the outer marker, the landing gear was extended and flaps were lowered full, at 50 degrees. The tower cleared TWA 5787 to land. The Instructor-Pilot answered, "Okay, we'll take the option" to make a full-stop landing, make a touch-and-go landing, or make only a low approach. The tower replied, "Roger, cleared."

1231:14.5

ATLANTIC CITY
  TOWER:

And 5787 is cleared to land, the wind one three zero degrees at five.

1231:15

INSTRUCTOR-
  PILOT:

Okay, we'll take the option.

1231:17

ATLANTIC CITY
  TOWER:

Roger, cleared.

1231:19

CAPTAIN:

Five hundred feet.

1231:20

INSTRUCTOR-
  PILOT:

Okay. Airspeed good . . . sink rate good . . . slightly right . . . right on the money, Harry.

1231:58

CAPTAIN:

Hundred to go.

INSTRUCTOR-
  PILOT:

Okay, missed approach.

1232:02

CAPTAIN:

Twenty-five flap.

INSTRUCTOR-
  PILOT:

Twenty-five flap. (SOUND OF ENGINE SPOOLUP.)

1232:08

CAPTAIN:

Takeoff power.

1232:09

INSTRUCTOR-
  PILOT:

Okay

1232:10

CAPTAIN:

Up gear. (SOUNDS OF TRIM ACTUATION AND MOVEMENT OF LANDING-GEAR LEVER.)

1232:12

INSTRUCTOR-
  PILOT:

Straight ahead to fifteen hundred feet.

CAPTAIN:

Right. (SOUND OF TRIM ACTUATION.)

1232:16

AN OBSERVING
  CAPTAIN (ON
  FLIGHT DECK):

Oh! Oh! Your hydraulic system's zeroed.

1232:17.5

CAPTAIN: What was that?

1232:18

INSTRUCTOR-
 PILOT: Oh . . .

CAPTAIN: Got no hydraulics?

FLIGHT ENGINEER: [Just] went down.

INSTRUCTOR-
 PILOT: They're all [out].

CAPTAIN: All of 'em out?

INSTRUCTOR-
 PILOT: Yeah.

1232:20

CAPTAIN: Pumps off.

1232:21

ATLANTIC CITY
 TOWER: Trans World, you gonna work Approach Control?

1232:24

INSTRUCTOR-PILOT
 (TO ATLANTIC
 CITY TOWER): Ah, stand by, we're having a hydraulic problem here.

1232:29

OBSERVING PILOT
 (ON FLIGHT
 DECK): Must have been, ah, after the gear was down already.

1232:32

INSTRUCTOR-
 PILOT: Well, the gear is still in the up [position].

CAPTAIN: No, gear's up. It may be that gear, ah . . . might be pumping it out in the up position.

1232:38

INSTRUCTOR-
 PILOT: Let's see, the gear is down. (SOUND OF LANDING GEAR LEVER MOVEMENT.) I'm gonna put it down again.

CAPTAIN: Yeah.

1232:41

INSTRUCTOR-
 PILOT: You got that? (SOUND OF ''POP'' LIKE THAT OF AN EN-GINE COMPRESSOR STALL.)

1232:43

INSTRUCTOR-
PILOT:

What happened? (BACKGROUND SCREAMING. STALL WARNING ALARM——STICKSHAKER——BEGINS AND LASTS FOR FIVE SECONDS.)

1232:44.5

CAPTAIN:

Give me that engine! (SOUND OF ENGINE SPOOL-DOWN.)

1232:46

INSTRUCTOR-
PILOT:

Harry . . . we're over!

1232:48

CAPTAIN:

Give me the engine!

1232:48.4

ATLANTIC CITY
TOWER:

Ah, look out!

1232:50

INSTRUCTOR-
PILOT:

We're over.

(SOUND OF IMPACT.)

Flight 5787 had entered a steep, descending right turn and hit the aircraft parking ramp adjacent to the airfield's hangar. All five persons aboard the aircraft received fatal injuries. The aircraft was destroyed.

14. *Texas International Airlines Flight 655 (TTA 655)*

On 27 September 1973, Texas International's Flight 655, a Convair 600, with a crew of three and eight passengers, departed Eldorado at 2015 Central Daylight Time destined for Pine Bluff, Arkansas. After takeoff, the aircraft flew a heading of 290 degrees and climbed to an altitude of 1,500 feet. The flight operated at altitudes up to 3,000 feet. The minimum altitudes for Flight 655's route varied from 2,200 feet at Eldorado to 4,500 feet. The Captain gave heading and altitude orders to the First Officer, who was flying the aircraft.

FIRST OFFICER:	Yeah?
CAPTAIN:	That might not be a hole there [in the clouds].
FIRST OFFICER:	We know shortly. It sorta looks like twenty-four miles to the end. I don't mind, do you?
CAPTAIN:	I don't care, just as long as we don't go through it [the weather].
FIRST OFFICER:	Looks a little strange through there, looks like something attenuating through there. It's shadow.
CAPTAIN:	Yeah, looks like a shadow. Is that better?
FIRST OFFICER:	Naw, I don't care.
CAPTAIN:	Suit yourself.
FIRST OFFICER:	Well, I don't know, looks a little light in here, this thing hits your eyeballs pretty hard.
CAPTAIN:	That's what I'm holding this thing for.
FIRST OFFICER:	That's all right, it doesn't hurt if she's bright.
CAPTAIN:	As long as you've got it.

FIRST OFFICER:	See something?
CAPTAIN:	I think it's snow.
FIRST OFFICER:	I still think that's a shadow.
CAPTAIN:	I do, too.
FIRST OFFICER:	Wanna go around [the weather front]?
CAPTAIN:	Yeah, why not.
FIRST OFFICER:	All right.
CAPTAIN:	I'd slow it up a little bit too. Good chance.
FIRST OFFICER:	What we got, decreasing . . .
CAPTAIN:	I didn't hear you.
FIRST OFFICER:	The visibility is dropping.
CAPTAIN:	Yeah.
FIRST OFFICER:	Well . . . rain.
CAPTAIN:	Raining [all over the place]. You got something down there?
FIRST OFFICER:	The other one's a rain data, look at it.
CAPTAIN:	Yeah, it's probably getting ground clutter down there. That's ground . . .
FIRST OFFICER:	What's all this, lights, in those fields? What the hell are they, chicken farms?
CAPTAIN:	Yeah.
FIRST OFFICER:	God Almighty. They're planning on growing a few eggs, ain't they?
CAPTAIN:	Yep, that's what they are.
FIRST OFFICER:	What the hell have I got there, ya know? I thought the end of that line was way back down over there, now. . . . It's a [the cloud is a] real cute l'il old curlicue, ain't it?
CAPTAIN:	Yeah, ha, ha! There's not much to that, but we gotta stay away from it. . . .
FIRST OFFICER:	I can't get this stupid radar. . . . You got any idea where we're at?
CAPTAIN:	Yeah, two sixteen'll take us right to the VOR.
FIRST OFFICER:	Two, ah . . .
CAPTAIN:	Two zero nine, I got. . . .
FIRST OFFICER:	Fifteen [thousand feet] . . .
CAPTAIN:	I'm not concerned with that [their altitude]. I could care less.
FIRST OFFICER:	I guess you're right. That, that is just extending on and on and on as we go along 'cause it hasn't

moved in about three or four miles in the last thirty minutes, it seems like.

CAPTAIN: I guess it's building up that way [now]. (SOUND OF WHISTLING.) What's Hot Springs?

FIRST OFFICER: Sir?

CAPTAIN: What's Hot Springs's VOR? Is it ten zero, is that right?

FIRST OFFICER: Yeah, yeah, ah, that's right. We don't want to get too far up the . . . it gets hilly.

CAPTAIN: Yeah . . . stars are shining. Why don't you try two thousand? If we got up here anywhere near Hot Springs, we get in the damned mountains.

FIRST OFFICER: Ah, you reckon there's a ridge line along here somewhere? Go down five hundred feet, you can see all kindsa lights. Let's go ahead and try for twenty-five hundred.

CAPTAIN: All right. Fred, you can quit worrying about the mountains 'cause that'll clear everything over there.

FIRST OFFICER: That's why I wanted to go to twenty-five hundred feet. That's the Hot Springs highway right here, I think.

CAPTAIN: You 'bout right.

FIRST OFFICER: Texarkan . . . naw, it ain't, either. Texarkana's back here.

CAPTAIN: Texarkana's back over here somewhere.

FIRST OFFICER: Yeah. This ain't no Hot Springs highway.

CAPTAIN: Well, thirty degrees . . . thirty degrees takes you right to Texarkana, doesn't it? Hot Springs . . . here we are sittin' on fifty . . .

FIRST OFFICER: Yeah. Look how we're gainin' on the ground.

CAPTAIN: I don't know, Fred. Still we keep gettin' another one poppin' up every time . . . every time.

FIRST OFFICER: If we keep this up indefinitely, we'll be in Tulsa.

CAPTAIN: I haven't been in Tulsa for years.

FIRST OFFICER: Ha, ha, ha. The last time I was with Glen Duke, he said go whichever way you want to. I was going out of Abilene going to Dallas, took up a heading zero one zero and flew for about forty-five minutes, and he said, "Fred, you can't keep going on this, on this heading." I said "Why?" He said, "You gonna be in Oklahoma pretty

soon." I said, "I don't care if I'm in Oklahoma."
He said, "Fair enough." How'd I get all this airspeed?

CAPTAIN:	You're all right.
FIRST OFFICER:	[Pile it on.] We'll keep this speed here?
CAPTAIN:	A little while.
FIRST OFFICER:	There ain't no lights on the ground over there.
CAPTAIN:	Yeah, I see 'em behind us. See stars above us?
FIRST OFFICER:	I got some lights on the ground.
CAPTAIN:	There's just not many out here.
FIRST OFFICER:	Maybe . . . could be somethin' else, coach.
CAPTAIN:	Aha, we're gettin' rid of the clouds. We is in the clouds, Fred.
FIRST OFFICER:	Are we?
CAPTAIN:	Yeah. No, we're not. I can see above us. We got [ground] up ahead? I can see the ground here.
FIRST OFFICER:	Yeah, I can see the ground down here, too.
CAPTAIN:	Yeah . . . north is a fair heading, north.
FIRST OFFICER:	Now, what have we got here?
CAPTAIN:	Naw, you're all right. I can see some lights over here.
FIRST OFFICER:	I'll tell ya what, coach . . . that's probably Hot Springs.
CAPTAIN:	Yep, could be. Yeah, that might be either it or Arkadelphia.
FIRST OFFICER:	Well, I'm getting out of the clouds here, Mac, but I'm getting right straight into it.
CAPTAIN:	Oh, looks like you're all right.
FIRST OFFICER:	Do you see any stars above us? We're going in and outta some scud.
CAPTAIN:	Yeah, we've got a little bit here.
FIRST OFFICER:	I sure wish I knew where the hell we were.
CAPTAIN:	Well, I tell you what, we're, ah, on the two fifty . . . two sixty radial from, ah, Hot Springs.
FIRST OFFICER:	Figure I can kick her on up here. Maybe I can outrun it.
CAPTAIN:	I don't . . . I don't think you get up.
FIRST OFFICER:	Well, I, I got the damned thing pointed almost straight up to see what we got out here. Paintin' ridges and everything else, boss, and I'm not fa-miliar with the terrain. We're staying in the clouds.

CAPTAIN:	Yeah, I'd stay down. You're right in the . . . right in the base of the clouds. I tell you what, we're gonna be able to turn here in a minute.
FIRST OFFICER:	You wanna go through there?
CAPTAIN:	Yeah.
FIRST OFFICER:	All right. Good, looking good, Mac. Looking good.
CAPTAIN:	That's all right, wait a minute.
FIRST OFFICER:	Well, I can't even get, ah, Texarkana anymore.
CAPTAIN:	I'll tell you what, Fred . . .
FIRST OFFICER:	Okay, boss.
CAPTAIN:	Well, ah, we'll just try that, we'll try it. We're gonna be in the rain pretty soon. It's only about two miles wide.
FIRST OFFICER:	You tell me where you want me to go.
CAPTAIN:	Okay, give me a heading of, ah, three forty.
FIRST OFFICER:	Three forty?
CAPTAIN:	Three forty. Steady on. We got ten miles to go 'n' we're gonna turn . . . to the left about, ah, 'bout fifty degrees.
FIRST OFFICER:	Want me to turn, did ya say, fifty?
CAPTAIN:	Yeah, fifty left. On about, ah, two ninety.
FIRST OFFICER:	Two ninety.
CAPTAIN:	Ya got six miles to turn. Three miles south of turn.
FIRST OFFICER:	We're in it [the clouds].
CAPTAIN:	Huh?
FIRST OFFICER:	We're in solid, now.
CAPTAIN:	Are we?
FIRST OFFICER:	Hold it.
CAPTAIN:	Start your turn . . . standard rate. Level out and let me see it . . . when you hit two ninety.
FIRST OFFICER:	Aw, okay. There's your two ninety.
CAPTAIN:	Steady on. Should hit in about a half a mile. Should be out of it in 'bout two miles. You're in it. Are you through it? Turn thirty left.
FIRST OFFICER:	I can see the ground, now. There's thirty left. Naw, that's thirty-five. . . .
CAPTAIN:	Keep on truckin', just keep on a-truckin'.
FIRST OFFICER:	Well, we must be somewhere in Oklahoma.
CAPTAIN:	Doin' all the good in the world.

FIRST OFFICER:	Do you have any idea of what the frequency of the Paris VOR is?
CAPTAIN:	Put, ah, about two sixty-five, heading two sixty-five.
FIRST OFFICER:	Heading, two sixty-five. I would say we fucked up.
CAPTAIN:	Think so? (LAUGHTER.) Fred, descend to two thousand.
FIRST OFFICER:	Two thousand, coming down. Here we are, we're not out of it.
CAPTAIN:	Let's truck on. 'Bout five to the right. Shift over a little bit if you can.
FIRST OFFICER:	Sure can.
CAPTAIN:	That's all right. That's all right, you're doin all the good in the world. I thought we'd get, I thought it was moving that way on me only, we just kinda turned a little bit while you was looking at the map.
FIRST OFFICER:	Look.
CAPTAIN:	First time I ever made a mistake in my life.
FIRST OFFICER:	I'll be damned. Man, I wish I knew where we were so we'd have some idea of the general terrain around this damned place.
CAPTAIN:	I know what it is.
FIRST OFFICER:	What?
CAPTAIN:	That the highest point out here is about twelve hundred feet. The whole general area, and then we're not even where that is, I don't believe.
FIRST OFFICER:	I'll tell you what, as long as we travel northwest instead of west, and I still can't get Paris . . . (WHISTLING.)
CAPTAIN:	Go ahead and look at it. (WHISTLING.)
FIRST OFFICER:	Two hundred and fifty, we're about to pass over Page VOR. You know where that is?
CAPTAIN:	Yeah.
FIRST OFFICER:	All right.
CAPTAIN:	About a hundred and eighty degrees to Texarkana.
FIRST OFFICER:	About a hundred and fifty-two. Minimum en route altitude here is forty-four hund . . .

(SOUND OF IMPACT.)

Flight 655 crashed into the steep, heavily wooded north slope of Black Fork Mountain in the Ouachita Mountain Range at an elevation of 2,025 feet, about 600 feet below the top of the ridge. The three crew members and eight passengers of Flight 655 suffered fatal injuries. The aircraft was destroyed.

15. *United Airlines Flight 266*
(UAL 266)

On 18 January 1969, United Airlines Flight 266, a Boeing 727-22C, was scheduled to fly thirty-two passengers from Los Angeles to Milwaukee with a stop in Denver. The crew of six knew that the aircraft had an inoperative Number Three generator, but UAL's dispatcher cleared the aircraft with only two generators operable. The flight started its takeoff roll on Runway 24 at approximately 1817.

1816:58
L.A. TOWER: United 266, cleared for takeoff.

1817:00
FIRST OFFICER: United 266, rolling.

CAPTAIN (TO SEC-   Last three items [in check list].
    OND OFFICER):

SECOND OFFICER: Engine start switches. Anti-skid.
FIRST OFFICER: On.

1817:20.5
CAPTAIN: Takeoff thrust.
FIRST OFFICER: Set. Looks good.

1817:37
FIRST OFFICER: One hundred [knots per hour]. One ten. One twenty. Vee-R. Vee-two.

CAPTAIN: Gear up.
FIRST OFFICER: Gear up.

1817:55
L.A. TOWER: United 266, contact Departure Control.

1818:09

CAPTAIN: [You handle these things] light on the controls.

FIRST OFFICER: Yeah.

CAPTAIN: Flaps, ah, five . . . ?

FIRST OFFICER: Five. United 266, on departure.

LOS ANGELES DEPARTURE CONTROL: United 266, Los Angeles Departure Control radar contact, turn right heading two seven zero report leaving three thousand.

1818:21

FIRST OFFICER: Two seven zero, wilco.

1818:26.5

CAPTAIN: You have a green two.

FIRST OFFICER: Two.

1818:30 (SOUNDING OF WARNING BELL.)

1818:32.5

CAPTAIN: What the hell was that?

1818:34

FIRST OFFICER: Number One fire warning, Arn. . . .

1818:36

CAPTAIN: Okay, let's take care of the . . . warning.

1818:40

FIRST OFFICER: Pull it back for you?

1818:42

CAPTAIN: Yeah, pull it back.

FIRST OFFICER: Okay. (SOUND OF WARNING HORN.) That puts us on one generator too.

CAPTAIN: Huh?

FIRST OFFICER: That'll put us on one generator.

CAPTAIN: Yeah, watch that electrical loading.

FIRST OFFICER: Everything off?

1818:58

FIRST OFFICER: Ah, Departure, United 266.

1819:04

LOS ANGELES
  DEPARTURE
  CONTROL:

United 266, go ahead.

FIRST OFFICER:

Ah, we've had a fire warning on Number One engine we shut down. We'd like to come back.

1819:10

LOS ANGELES
  DEPARTURE
  CONTROL:

United 266, roger. What is your present altitude?

1819:13.5

(COCKPIT VOICE RECORDER OPERATION STOPPED.)

0000.00

(COCKPIT VOICE RECORDER RESUMED OPERATION AT AN
INDETERMINATE LATER TIME.)

0000.02

SECOND OFFICER:

We're gonna get screwed up. I don't know
[what's going on].

0000.06

FIRST OFFICER:

Keep it going up, Arnie. You're a thousand feet
. . . pull it up. . . .

(SOUND OF IMPACT.)

United Flight 266 crashed at approximately 1821, four minutes
after its initial takeoff roll, at a point 11.3 miles west of the airport
in the Pacific Ocean. The six crew members and the thirty-two
passengers suffered fatal injuries. The aircraft was destroyed.

16. *Allegheny Airlines Flight 485 (AL 485)*

ON 7 JUNE 1971, Allegheny Airlines Flight 485, an Allison Prop Jet Convair 340/440, with thirty passengers and a crew of three, departed the gate at 1333 Greenwich Mean Time, en route from Groton, Connecticut, to the Tweed–New Haven Airport via the Pond Point intersection.

1334:04

FIRST OFFICER: Quonset Approach, Allegheny, ah, 485's taxiing out of New London.

QUONSET POINT (SERVING GROTON TRAFFIC) APPROACH CONTROL: Allegheny 485, have your clearance, ready to copy?

FIRST OFFICER: Yeah, go ahead.

1334:13

QUONSET POINT APPROACH: Allegheny 485 is cleared to the Pond Point intersection via Groton two six seven degree radial to Saybrook Victor sixteen to intercept the Bridgeport zero nine nine radial to Pond Point, maintain four thousand.

1334:27

FIRST OFFICER: Understand we're cleared to Pond Point intersection, that's by the Groton two sixty-seven radial to Saybrook, intercept Victor sixteen and Victor sixteen to intercepting the zero nine nine degrees of Bridgeport to Pond Point, maintain four thousand. Did you get the readback?

1334:53

QUONSET POINT APPROACH: Allegheny 485, roger, your readback is correct, you are released [for takeoff].

FIRST OFFICER: Rog.

1334:58

QUONSET POINT APPROACH: And report [when] airborne.

1335:33

FIRST OFFICER: Four, eight, nine and one twenty-nine . . . New London, times are twenty-one, twenty-three, thirty-three, thirty-five. Put us over at, ah, New Haven, make 'em about, ah, fifty-two.

NEW LONDON: Twenty-one, twenty-three, thirty-three, thirty-five, New Haven at fifty-two, see you later.

FIRST OFFICER: Okay, we'll see ya.

1345:17

WESTCHESTER APPROACH: And Allegheny 485, at your nine o'clock position and five miles now is company inbound to New Haven.

FIRST OFFICER: Yes, sir, we have him.

1345:26

WESTCHESTER APPROACH: Okay, what's your altitude now, sir?

FIRST OFFICER: Out of three point five.

WESTCHESTER APPROACH: Okay, fine, thank you.

1345:30

FIRST OFFICER: Okay, ah, the visibility is good to the north of New Haven.

WESTCHESTER APPROACH: Fine, sir, thank you.

CAPTAIN: Yeah, that Dave, he keeps, keeps on runnin' ahead of us.

1345:54

FIRST OFFICER: New Haven, 485.

NEW HAVEN TOWER: Roger, 485.

1346:30

CAPTAIN: When he talks to you again tell him . . .

WESTCHESTER APPROACH: Allegheny 485, descend to one six hundred.

1346:35

FIRST OFFICER: Okay, we're going down to sixteen hundred, Allegheny 485.

1346:38

CAPTAIN: We'll take a turn at Pond Point.

WESTCHESTER APPROACH: 485, roger, make it New Haven weather sky partially obscured, one and three quarters in fog, wind one eight zero degrees at five, altimeter two niner niner seven.

1346:47

FIRST OFFICER: Okay, sir, and we'll take a turn right at the Point if that'll be all right.

WESTCHESTER APPROACH: Okay, you want to turn right into the airport?

1346:52

FIRST OFFICER: Yeah, that'll be okay at, ah, Pond Point be fine.

1346:55

WESTCHESTER APPROACH: Okay, I didn't get the latter part of that, turn right heading three six zero.

1346:59

FIRST OFFICER: Three six zero, Allegheny 485.

1347:01

WESTCHESTER APPROACH: Okay and you can intercept the final approach course on that heading. You'll be right at Pond Point. You're cleared for a VOR approach.

1347:06

FIRST OFFICER: Okay, thank you, sir. Cleared for the approach, Allegheny 485.

WESTCHESTER APPROACH: Roger, you're welcome.

CAPTAIN: What was that wind, do you remember offhand?

FIRST OFFICER: A hundred and eighty at five.

1347:25

WESTCHESTER APPROACH: Okay, and Allegheny 485 contact New Haven Tower one two four point eight now. You're Pond Point inbound.

1347:30.1

FIRST OFFICER: Okay, twenty-four eight, thank you a lot.

WESTCHESTER APPROACH:	You're welcome, sir.

1347:34.7
CAPTAIN: Before you talk to him, will you give me fifteen [degrees of flaps] and gear down, please? (SOUND OF LANDING GEAR.)

1347:40.4
FIRST OFFICER: There ya go. New Haven Tower, Allegheny 485 is, ah, passin' the Point comin' inbound.

1347:53.9
NEW HAVEN TOWER: Roger, 485, runway your choice, sir. The wind is nine zero degrees at five, altimeter two niner niner six, Runway 2 or 20.

1348:01.1
CAPTAIN: Well, tell him, ah, well that's all right. We'll take [Runway] 2.

1348:04.7
FIRST OFFICER: Okay, the way it looks we'll take 2. [It'll] be all right.

1348:07.5
NEW HAVEN TOWER: Roger, cleared to land Runway 2.

1348:11.2
CAPTAIN: Out of a thousand [feet].

1348:17.9
CAPTAIN AND FIRST OFFICER: . . . Gear down. (FINAL CHECKLIST ITEMS, CHALLENGE AND RESPONSE, BOTH VOICES SIMULTANEOUSLY.)

CAPTAIN: Give me forty [degrees flaps]. I'm telling you . . .

1348:32.2
FIRST OFFICER: Out of five hundred [feet]. Looks about a hundred feet atop [a one-hundred-foot ceiling].

1348:35.3
CAPTAIN: They sure do.

1348:37.0
FIRST OFFICER: Not very good, is it? Top minimums. [Pause] I don't have it. Decision height. . . . You got a hundred and five, sinkin' five. . . .

CAPTAIN: All right. Keep a real sharp eye out here. . . .

FIRST OFFICER: Okay. Oh, this . . . is low. You can't see through this stuff.

1349:20.5

CAPTAIN: I can see the water. I got [it sighted] straight down.

1349:23.8

FIRST OFFICER: Ah, yeah, I can see the water. We're right over the water! Man, we ain't twenty feet off the water. . . . Hold it.

1349:30.9 (SOUND OF IMPACT.)

Allegheny Flight 485 struck a row of beach cottages at an altitude of 29 feet at a distance of 4,890 feet from the threshold of Runway 2. Twenty-eight passengers and two crew members were fatally injured. Two passengers and the First Officer survived. The aircraft was destroyed.

17. Eastern Airlines Flight 401 (EAL 401)

ON 29 DECEMBER 1972, Eastern Airlines Flight 401, a Lockheed L-1011, departed JFK International Airport bound for the Miami International Airport with 163 passengers and 13 crew members on board. The regularly scheduled flight was uneventful until the approach to Miami, when the landing-gear handle was placed in the down position but the green light in the cockpit, which would have indicated to the flight crew that the nose landing gear was fully extended and locked, failed to illuminate. The Captain tried repeatedly to lower the landing gear, but the green "gear-down" indicator still failed to light.

2332:19
MIAMI APPROACH: Eastern 401, left heading, one zero zero three from the marker, cleared to ILS 9 Left approach, tower one one eight point three, good morning.

2332:26
CAPTAIN: One one eight point three, Eastern 401, so long.

2332:35
CAPTAIN: Miami Tower, Eastern 401 just turned on final [landing approach].

2332:52
CAPTAIN: Miami Tower, do you read, Eastern 401 just turned on final?

2332:56
MIAMI TOWER: Eastern 401 heavy, continue approach to 9 Left.

2333:00
CAPTAIN: Continue approach, roger.

2333:00.5

SECOND OFFICER:	Continuous ignition. No smoke.
CAPTAIN:	Coming on.
SECOND OFFICER:	Brake system.
CAPTAIN:	Okay.
SECOND OFFICER:	Radar.
CAPTAIN:	Up, off.
SECOND OFFICER:	Hydraulic panels checked.
FIRST OFFICER:	Thirty-five [degrees flaps], thirty-five.
CAPTAIN:	Bert, is that handle in?
SECOND OFFICER:	Engine cross bleeds are open.

2333:22

FIRST OFFICER:	Gear down.
CAPTAIN:	I gotta . . .
FIRST OFFICER:	No nose gear.

2333:25

CAPTAIN:	I gotta raise it back up.

2333:47

CAPTAIN:	Now I'm gonna try it down one more time.
FIRST OFFICER:	All right. (SOUND OF ALTITUDE ALERT HORN.) Right gear. Well, want to tell 'em we'll take it around and circle around and . . . around?

2334:05

CAPTAIN (TO MIAMI TOWER):	Well, ah, tower, this is Eastern, ah, 401. It looks like we're gonna have to circle. We don't have a light on our nose gear yet.

2334:14

MIAMI TOWER:	Eastern 401 heavy, roger. Pull up, climb straight ahead to two thousand, go back to Approach Control, one twenty-six.

2334:19

FIRST OFFICER:	Twenty-two degrees. Twenty-two degrees, gear up.
CAPTAIN:	Put power on it first, Bert. Thatta boy. Leave the damn gear down till we find out what we got [wrong].
FIRST OFFICER:	All right.

SECOND OFFICER:	You want me to test the [green] lights or not?
CAPTAIN:	Yeah.
FIRST OFFICER (TO CAPTAIN):	Ah, Bob, it might be the light [that is malfunctioning]. Could you jiggle the, the light?
SECOND OFFICER:	It's [the light] gotta, gotta come out a' little bit and then snap in.
CAPTAIN (TO MIAMI TOWER):	Okay, going up to two thousand, one twenty-eight six.

2334:58

FIRST OFFICER:	We're up to two thousand. [To the Captain]: You want me to fly it, Bob?
CAPTAIN:	What frequency did he want us on, Bert?
FIRST OFFICER:	One twenty-eight six.
CAPTAIN:	I'll talk to 'em.
SECOND OFFICER:	[Speaking of the indicator light): I can't make it pull out, either.
CAPTAIN:	We got pressure.
SECOND OFFICER:	Yes, sir, all systems.

2335:09

CAPTAIN:	All right, ah, Approach Control, Eastern 401, we're right over the airport here and climbing to two thousand feet. In fact, we've just reached two thousand feet and we've got to get a green light on our nose gear.

2335:20

MIAMI APPROACH:	Eastern 401, roger. Turn left heading three six zero and maintain two thousand, vectors to 9 Left final.
CAPTAIN:	Left three six zero.

2336:04

CAPTAIN:	Put the . . . on autopilot here.
SECOND OFFICER:	All right.
CAPTAIN:	See if you can get that light out.
FIRST OFFICER:	All right.
CAPTAIN:	Now push the switches just a . . . forward. Okay. You got it sideways, then. Naw, I don't think it'll fit. You gotta turn it one quarter turn to the left [referring to the faulty indicator light].

2336:27

MIAMI APPROACH: Eastern 401, turn left heading three zero zero.

CAPTAIN: Okay. Three zero zero, Eastern 401.

2337:08

CAPTAIN: Hey, hey, get down there [in the nose-wheel well] and see if that damn nose wheel's down. You better do that.

FIRST OFFICER: You got a handkerchief or something so I can get a little better grip on this [indicator light]? Anything I can do with it?

CAPTAIN: Get down there and see if that, see if that damned thing . . .

FIRST OFFICER: This [light] won't come out, Bob. If I had a pair of pliers, I could cushion it with that Kleenex.

SECOND OFFICER: I can give you pliers but if you force it, you'll break it, just believe me.

FIRST OFFICER: Yeah, I'll cushion it with Kleenex.

SECOND OFFICER: Oh, we can give you pliers.

2337:48

MIAMI APPROACH: Eastern, ah, 401, turn left heading two seven zero.

2337:53

CAPTAIN: Left two seven zero, roger.

2338:34

CAPTAIN: To hell with it, to hell with this. Go down and see if it's lined up with the red line. That's all we care. [Don't screw] around with that damned twenty-cent piece of light equipment we got on this [panel].

2338:46

CAPTAIN: Eastern 401 . . . ah, one'll go, ah, out west just a little further if we can here and, ah, see if we can get this light to come on here.

2338:54

MIAMI APPROACH: All right, ah, we got you headed westbound there now, Eastern 401.

2338:56

CAPTAIN: All right. [To Second Officer]: How much fuel we got left on this . . . ?

SECOND OFFICER:	Fifty-two five.
FIRST OFFICER:	[About the indicator light]: It won't come out, no way.

2339:37

CAPTAIN:	We can tell if that [gear's] down by looking down at our indices. I'm sure it's down. There's no way it couldn't help but be.
FIRST OFFICER:	I'm sure it is.
CAPTAIN:	It free falls down.
FIRST OFFICER:	The tests don't show that the lights worked, anyway.
CAPTAIN:	That's right.
FIRST OFFICER:	It's a faulty light.

2341:05

FIRST OFFICER:	Bob, this [light] just won't come out.
CAPTAIN:	All right, just leave it there.
SECOND OFFICER:	I don't see it [the wheel] down there.
CAPTAIN:	Huh?
SECOND OFFICER:	I don't see it.
CAPTAIN:	You can see that the indis . . . for the nose wheel, ah, there's a place in there you can look and see if they're lined up. . . .
SECOND OFFICER:	I know. A little like a telescope.
CAPTAIN:	Yeah.
SECOND OFFICER:	Well . . .
CAPTAIN:	It's not lined up?
SECOND OFFICER:	I can't see it. It's pitch dark and I throw the little light I get, ah, nothing.

2341:31

CAPTAIN:	[Are the] well-wheel lights on?
SECOND OFFICER:	Pardon?
CAPTAIN:	Well-wheel lights on?
SECOND OFFICER:	Yeah, well-wheel lights always on if the gear's down.
CAPTAIN:	Now try it.

2341:40

MIAMI APPROACH:	Eastern 401, how are things coming along out there?

2341:44

CAPTAIN: Okay. We'd like to turn around and come, come back in. Clear on left.

MIAMI APPROACH: Eastern 401, turn left heading one eight zero.

2341:50

CAPTAIN: Huh?

2342:05

FIRST OFFICER: [We did] something to the altitude.

CAPTAIN: What?

2342:07

FIRST OFFICER: We're still at two thousand, right?

2342:09

CAPTAIN: Hey, what's happening here? I . . .

2342:12   (SOUND OF IMPACT.)

Eastern 401 had failed to monitor the flight instruments and to detect the descent soon enough to prevent impact with the ground. Preoccupation with the nose landing gear allowed the descent to go unnoticed. The aircraft crashed at 2342 Eastern Standard Time, 18.7 miles west-northwest of Miami International Airport. Of the 163 passengers and 13 crew members aboard, 94 passengers and 5 crew members received fatal injuries. The aircraft was destroyed.

18. *Mohawk Airlines Flight 40 (MOH 40)*

ON 23 JUNE 1967, Mohawk Flight 40, a British Aircraft Corporation BAC 1-11, was a regularly scheduled passenger flight from Syracuse, New York, to Washington, D.C., with a stop at Elmira, New York. The flight from Syracuse to Elmira was routine. Before takeoff for Washington, with thirty passengers and a crew of four, Flight 40 received an Instrument Flight Rules (IFR) clearance to Washington's National Airport. Flight 40 lifted off Runway 24 at 1439:40. The tower controllers noticed nothing unusual about the aircraft or its maneuvering. At 1444:11, New York Center cleared Flight 40 to climb to 16,000 feet. At 1447:00, the radar blip of Flight 40 appeared to slow down for one sweep, then move laterally for one sweep, and finally to disappear from the scope.

1443:52

CAPTAIN (TO FIRST OFFICER): I can't see a thing out there, Troy.

SECOND OFFICER: Neither can I.

1444:11

NEW YORK CENTER: Ah, Mohawk 40, climb now and maintain one six thousand.

1444:12

CAPTAIN: Ahhhhh . . . we're not gonna have that!

1444:19

FIRST OFFICER: Well, folks, here we go again.

1444:24

CAPTAIN: Ah, 40, climb to and maintain si . . . say again. What?

FIRST OFFICER: One six thousand.

1444:33
FIRST OFFICER: Ah, feel . . . it's not doing that exactly. . . . It's hard to tell just what it is.

1444:41
CAPTAIN: Ah, let's see . . . pull back on your speed.

FIRST OFFICER: Wait a minute, I'm doing it. Hey, there's something screwy here.

CAPTAIN: I know it.

1444:49
CAPTAIN (TO NEW YORK CENTER): Ah, Mohawk 40 is having a little control problem here. Well, ah, we'll advise you, ah, we may have to declare an emergency.

FIRST OFFICER: Yeah, that's gonna be [necessary].

1445:04
CAPTAIN: I got it. I got it.

FIRST OFFICER: Righto.

CAPTAIN: Tell 'em we're unable to maintain six thousand, goin' back to Elmira.

FIRST OFFICER: We're making a one eight back to Elmira?

CAPTAIN: To Elmira, six thousand.

1445:14
FIRST OFFICER: Ah, New York, Mohawk, ah, New York, Mohawk 40, like to return to Elmira, ah, ah, six thousand.

1445:16
CAPTAIN: We lost all control. . . . We don't have anything!

FIRST OFFICER: We're in manual [control] now.

1445:27
CAPTAIN: Yeah, but I can't do anything!

FIRST OFFICER: Well, okay.

1445:42
CAPTAIN: Let's go up for a minute. Here we go, easy now, easy.

1445:54
FIRST OFFICER: Looks like everything's the matter.

1446:02
CAPTAIN:

Pull back! Pull back! Keep workin'. We're makin' it. Pull back, straight now. Climb now. That's it, easy now. Now cut the gun, cut the gun, we're in now.

1446:23
FIRST OFFICER:

Ooooooh-weee! I don't like that.

1446:31
CAPTAIN:

Ah, we better turn back toward Elmira. Now wait a minute, wait, ah, let's go straight ahead.

FIRST OFFICER:

Okay.

1446:37
CAPTAIN:

What have we done to that damn tail surface, ya have any idea?

FIRST OFFICER:

I don't know, ah, I, I just can't figure it out.

1446:44
FIRST OFFICER:

Ah, we've lost both systems.

CAPTAIN:

Both?

1446:47
CAPTAIN:

I can't keep this . . . from . . . all right, I'm gonna use both hands now.

FIRST OFFICER:

Okay.

CAPTAIN:

Both hands. Pull her back! Pull 'er . . . [unintelligible] . . . power!

1446:55
CAPTAIN:

Both hands, back, both hands! *Pull Back!*

1447:11
CAPTAIN:

I've gone out of control!

1447:17

(SOUND OF IMPACT.)

A fire had destroyed the pitch control systems, causing Flight 40 to crash. All passengers and crew received fatal injuries. The aircraft was destroyed.

19. *Eastern Airlines Flight 212 (EAL 212)*

ON 11 SEPTEMBER 1974, Eastern Airlines flight 212, a Douglas DC-9-31, was operating as a scheduled passenger flight from Charleston, South Carolina, to Chicago, with a stop at Charlotte, North Carolina. The flight, with seventy-eight passengers and a crew of four, departed Charleston at 1100 Greenwich Mean Time. At 1125:01, Atlanta Control cleared the flight to contact Charlotte. At 1125:18, Charlotte Approach Control directed Flight 212 to "fly heading zero four zero, vectors to VOR, final approach course Runway 36, descend and maintain six thousand [feet]." The Captain acknowledged the clearance, then completed the landing checklist and announced, "In-range." The First Officer, who was flying the aircraft, responded, "Okay."

1128:30 GMT

CAPTAIN (CHATTING WITH THE FIRST OFFICER): Oh, yeah, after . . .

FIRST OFFICER: . . . elected representatives.

1128:34

CAPTAIN: Right, I heard this morning on the news while I was . . .

1128:37

CAPTAIN: . . . might stop proceedings against impeachment [of the President]. . . . (BEEP SOUND OF ALTITUDE ALERT.)

1128:44

CAPTAIN: . . . because you can't have a pardon for Nixon and the Watergate people.

1128:49
CAPTAIN: . . . Old Ford's beginning to take some of his hard knocks. . . .

1128:53
ATLANTA CONTROL: Eastern 212, turn left heading two four zero.

1128:57
CAPTAIN: Two four zero, Eastern 212, we're at six [thousand feet].

1129:00
ATLANTA CONTROL: Eastern 212 . . .

1129:02
CAPTAIN: All right down to four [thousand feet].

1129:05
FIRST OFFICER: Fifteen degrees [flaps], please.

1129:14
ATLANTA CONTROL: Eastern 212, contact Charlotte Approach one one niner point zero.

1129:18
CAPTAIN: One nineteen nothing, good day. Charlotte Approach, Eastern 212, descending to four [thousand]. We're turning to two forty.

1129:34
CHARLOTTE APPROACH: Eastern 212, continue heading two four zero, descend and maintain three thousand [feet].

1128:38
CAPTAIN: All right, on down to three.

1129:46
FIRST OFFICER: One thing that kills me is the damned mess and all that's going on now. We should be taking some definite direction to save the country. Arabs are taking over every damned thing. They bought . . . hell, they got so much real estate, so much land, they bought an island for seventeen million dollars off Carolina. They . . .

1130.01
FIRST OFFICER: . . . The stock market and the damned Swiss are going to sink our damned money, gold over there . . . (SOUND OF PITCH TRIM.)

1130:32
CAPTAIN: Yes, sir, boy. They got the money, don't they? They got so much damned money.

1130:35
FIRST OFFICER: That stuff is coming in at such a fantastic rate. . . . Yeah, I think, damn if we don't do something by nineteen eighty, they'll [the Arabs] own the world.

CAPTAIN: They owned it all, at one time.

1130:43
FIRST OFFICER: That's right.

1130:46
FIRST OFFICER: I'll be willing to go back to one . . . to one car . . . any, ah, a lot of other restrictions if we can get something going.

1130:52
CAPTAIN: Yeah.

1130:59
CAPTAIN: I'm car poor. I got, well . . . I just got two [cars] now. I just gave one to my boy, but I'm buying this new one.

1131:09
CHARLOTTE APPROACH: Eastern 212, turn right, reading three five zero, cleared VOR three six approach. You're six miles south of Ross intersection.

1131:15
CAPTAIN: Okay, three fifty, cleared for approach.

1131:36
CAPTAIN: There's Carowinds [intersection], I think that's what that is.

1131:39
CHARLOTTE APPROACH: Eastern 212, you resume normal speed, tower one eighteen one.

1131:42
CAPTAIN: One eighteen one, two twelve, good day. Hello, ah, Charlotte Tower, it's Eastern 212. We're about five miles south of Ross.

1131:51
CHARLOTTE   Eastern 212, continue number two.
  TOWER:

1133:17
CAPTAIN: There's, ah, Ross. Now we can go on down.

1133.22
FIRST OFFICER: How about fifty degrees [flaps], please.

1133:25
CAPTAIN: Fifty. [To Charlotte Tower]: Eastern 212 by Ross.

1133:44
CHARLOTTE   Eastern 212, clear to land, three six.
  TOWER:

1133:52
CAPTAIN: Yeah, we're all ready. All we got to do is find the airport.

1133:58   (SOUND OF IMPACT.)

The aircraft struck trees, broke up, and burst into flames about 1.75 miles from Ross intersection and about 3.3 miles short of the threshold of Runway 36. The crew's lack of altitude awareness during the approach was the probable cause of the crash. Of the eighty-two people on board, ten passengers and two crew members survived. The aircraft was destroyed.

Glossary

Anti-skid: A device used after the aircraft has touched down that senses the loss of wheel traction and automatically releases and reapplies brakes, thus preventing the aircraft from skidding on a wet or icy runway.

Approach Plate: A chart containing data on a certain runway—elevation, length, and heading—necessary for the pilot to make a safe landing.

APU: Auxiliary Power Unit, an engine aboard the aircraft, usually located in the tail, for the generation of electrical and hydraulic power when the main engines are shut off.

Bug: A setting on the rim of several instruments in the cockpit to remind the pilot of reference speeds and altitudes.

Chocks: Metal braces placed in front and behind the wheels of the main landing gear when the aircraft is parked.

Cross Bleeds: Use of heated air in a jet engine to pressurize and heat the cabin and operate pneumatic systems; when bleeds in the engine are open, air is supplied to these systems.

Cross Feeds: Valves that permit the transfer of fuel from one tank to another.

Cut the gun: Reduce power.

Five-by: A perfect degree of hearing clarity, as in, "I read you five-by."

Glide Slope Capture: On an Instrument Landing System approach to a runway, when the pilot has captured the glide slope the aircraft is at the proper altitude and on a correct heading for a safe landing.

Heavy: An Air Traffic Control term for a larger aircraft, usually a wide-bodied Boeing 747, DC-10, L-1011, but also in some instances a reference to a stretch DC-8.

Hole: An opening in the clouds.

Hydraulics: The ability to operate the control surfaces of the aircraft, as in, "Do we have hydraulics?"

Ident: Identify the aircraft to Air Traffic Control by pushing a button inside the cockpit that illuminates a dot on radar screens beside which are an ident number and altitude. Same as *squawk*.

Lap: An infant passenger who rides in a parent's lap.

Minimums: Levels of altitude and visibility below which the aircraft cannot safely fly.

Paint: As an object appears on a radar screen with each sweep of the antenna across the target or object; thus, an air traffic controller, for example, will radio a pilot that he is "painting" storm clouds on his radar screen and for the pilot to turn his aircraft on such-and-such heading to avoid the clouds.

Rabbit: A line of strobe lights at the threshold of runways that illuminate in rapid succession from the farthest away to the nearest to the end of the runway.

Read: Understand.

Rotate: Takeoff speed required, depending on the aircraft, its weight, etc., for the pilot to lift its nose off the runway. Used as a command to "rotate," or lift the nose when the required speed has been reached.

RVR: Runway Visual Range, the scientific measurement in feet of runway visibility, depending on such factors as fog, haze, smoke, dust, precipitation.

Scud: Low stratus clouds.

SIGMET: Significant Meteorological Advisory; usually indicating severe weather.

Slats: Devices on the leading edges of the wings used on takeoff and landing to increase the lift of the wings.

Spoilers: Small surfaces on the tops of the wings that are extended after touchdown to reduce or "spoil" the wings' lift and thus facilitate braking of the aircraft.

Spool: Increase or decrease the revs of an aircraft's turbine engines.

Spread: The difference between the temperature and the dew point, which tells the pilot the likelihood of fog, among other things.

Squawk: Same as Ident.

Stall: Airspeed at which the aircraft's wings can no longer maintain lift to prevent the aircraft from falling. To recover from a stall, the aircraft must have sufficient altitude to regain adequate airspeed by putting the nose down and diving.

Stickshaker: A warning device on commercial aircraft that literally shakes the control column in the pilot's hands to warn of the approach of the aircraft's stall speed.

Three Green: A phrase to indicate that the three landing gears are down and locked; indeed, in the cockpits of most aircraft there are three green lights.

Transponder: An electronic device aboard aircraft that communicates a signal to ATC radar, indicating on the radar screen an enhanced signal that includes an identifying number and the aircraft's altitude. Used in conjunction with the squawk and ident procedure.

Vector: Heading or direction; used as a verb or noun.

V-1: The aircraft's go- no-go decision speed on takeoff; if, for example, an engine fails at V-1, the takeoff is aborted.

V-2: The takeoff velocity that an aircraft must be able to maintain to clear a theoretical obstacle at the end of the runway, if one engine should fail to provide power.

VOR: A very high frequency omnidirectional range navigational aid.

V-R: Same as "rotation."

Wilco: Will comply, will do.